VOLUME II

I am your
JESUS of MERCY

Lessons and Messages
To The World
from
Our Lord and Our Lady

Published by
THE RIEHLE FOUNDATION
P.O. BOX 7
MILFORD, OHIO 45150

According to a decree of the Congregation for the Doctrine of the Faith, approved by H.H. Pope Paul VI, (1966), it is permitted to publish, without an imprimatur, texts relating to new revelations, apparitions, prophecies or miracles.

However, in accordance with the regulations of the Second Vatican Council, the publisher states that we do not wish to precede the judgment of the Church in this matter, to which we humbly submit.

Published by The Riehle Foundation
For additional copies, write:

The Riehle Foundation
P.O. Box 7
Milford, OH 45150

Library of Congress Catalog Card No.: 89-63546

ISBN: 1-877678-12-0

TABLE OF CONTENTS

Publisher's Foreword

In early December, 1989, the Riehle Foundation published the book *I Am Your Jesus Of Mercy.* 70,000 copies were distributed in seven months. The book, and its popularity, is a confirmation of the great spiritual hunger that exists in the world today.

I Am Your Jesus Of Mercy contains an introduction to the events at St. Maria Goretti Parish, and the "lessons" and "messages" from Our Lord and Our Lady allegedly being received there. The lessons are profound, re-affirm the Gospel teachings, echo the teachings of apparitions currently taking place around the world, particularly Medjugorje, Yugoslavia, and provide spiritual nourishment to a world woefully in need of Divine Mercy.

In this book, *I Am Your Jesus Of Mercy, Volume II,* the remaining lessons, sets Number 3 and 4, and the messages through the Spring of 1990 are printed. Fr. Jack Spaulding, Pastor of St. Maria Goretti Parish, had provided the introduction to the format of the events in Volume I. If the reader has not yet read the first volume, we would suggest that they do so.

Fr. Spaulding had explained that the **lessons** are received through one messenger, a member of the Thursday evening prayer group, and **messages** have also been received through other members of the group. Additional messages are sometimes given through Fr. Spaulding as part of the homily at the Thursday night liturgy.

The **lessons,** as received by the messenger, a young woman, (Gianna Talone-Bianchi), are for all the world and are allegedly received by the messenger from Our Lord in private, during prayer, and not as part of the prayer group meetings. They are dictated and written down as received. The **messages,** given to the Thursday evening prayer group, are received by two members; they are read at the Thursday liturgy, and are applicable to all people, though most often directed specifically to the original prayer group members. Specific messages, through Fr. Spaulding as part of the homily, occur at random dates and are generally directed to those in attendance.

In the Summer of 1989, The Most Reverend Thomas O'Brien, Bishop of the Diocese of Phoenix, established a commission to investigate the events occurring at St. Maria Goretti. In late October, 1989, the three member commission reported their conclusions and recommendations to Bishop O'Brien. The members of the commission were appointed because of their expertise in the areas of theology, spirituality and psychology, according to the Bishop.

The investigative commission neither approved nor condemned the events. Fr. Ernest Larkin, a member of the commission stated:

> "We don't think that these are hoaxes or that there is any attempt to deceive anybody. We simply maintain that there is not enough evidence to say that these are miracles. The events seem to us to be explained as human experiences and by ordinary human dynamics." Fr. Larkin further stated: "We're not saying that it's impossible that these are miracles, we're just saying that there's not enough evidence to say that these are miracles."

Bishop O'Brien responded to the commission's report by issuing a four-page statement, January 8, 1990. In the statement, Bishop O'Brien confirmed the report of the commission members regarding the participants of the prayer group, that: "There was no indication of deceit and that the individuals are people of great faith." In part, the text of the Bishop's statement included the following report:

"At the end of October 1989, the commission reported to me their conclusions and recommendations concerning the events at St. Maria Goretti Church. The commission concluded that the messages (locutions) are explainable within the range of ordinary human experience and obviously we cannot know for certain whether or not the locutions or visions are miraculous in the true sense of the word. By miraculous, we mean a mode of action beyond the ordinary laws of nature and caused by an exceptional, direct divine intervention.(. . .) The commission further stated that the commitment to the Lord and the depth of faith in all the individuals involved are beyond question. The commission also said that Father Spaulding has demonstrated himself to be a good priest and he should be commended for his devotion to Our Lady.

"After much prayerful discernment, I have accepted the conclusions drawn by the commission and I have personally communicated this decision to Fr. Spaulding."

Bishop O'Brien further listed and approved several recommendations of the commission concerning the events at St. Maria Goretti, including the continuation of the prayer meeting and liturgy on Thursday evenings, "but without any unequivocal claim of miraculous intervention in the absence of any external evidence that the messages are directly from Our Lord, or the Blessed Virgin Mary." He also stated his intention to establish a "Community of Discernment" to aid the prayer group in interpreting any future events and monitor the circulation of any publication. The Bishop concluded by commending Fr. Spaulding and the members of his prayer group for their spirit of prayerful cooperation.

As Publisher of this book, and the preceeding volume of *I Am Your Jesus Of Mercy,* we take no position as to warranting the authenticity of the events at St. Maria Goretti Parish. We do believe that the world now lives in the time of "Divine Mercy" and is in desperate need of hearing and reflecting on the Gospel truths forgotten or neglected by so many. Toward this end we offer this publication and will attempt to make it available to as many as possible without regard for profit.

In the meantime, and since the report of the commission and the Bishop's statement, the events at St. Maria Goretti continue. Since then, the messenger of the lessons (and occasionally another prayer group member) have claimed that they now receive apparitions as well. Special messages are also received. It is significant that the center of these events at St. Maria Goretti is PRAYER. Two hours of prayer every Thursday is further supported by several additional prayer groups. Teenagers and young adults are most noticeable at these meetings. There is a commitment there. It is a praying community. It is a "Center of Mercy."

Bill Reck
The Riehle Foundation

NOTE: The Publisher assumes full responsibility for this publication, without endorsement or promotion from the Archbishop and the Diocese of Phoenix, or from Fr. Spaulding and St. Maria Goretti Parish.

COME UNTO ME

The Chaplet of the Divine Mercy

(for private recitation on ordinary rosary beads)

Begin with:

Our Father..., Hail Mary..., The Apostles' Creed.

Then, on the OUR FATHER BEADS say the following words:

Eternal Father, I offer You the Body and Blood, Soul and Divinity of Your dearly beloved Son, Our Lord Jesus Christ, in atonement for our sins and those of the whole world.

On the HAIL MARY BEADS say the following words:

For the sake of His sorrowful Passion have mercy on us and on the whole world.

In conclusion, THREE TIMES recite these words:

Holy God, Holy Mighty One, Holy Immortal One, have mercy on us and on the whole world.

VOLUME II

Part I

Lessons From Jesus Christ, Our Lord, Given For the World

**Through The Messenger At
St. Maria Goretti Parish
Scottsdale, Arizona**

September 1989 through April 1990

Note:

Since all the words herein are those of Our Lord, as recorded from the messenger involved, quotation marks for each lesson are eliminated.

Lessons From Our Lord

MOTHER OF SORROWS

My dear people,

Your "Mother of Sorrows" not only lived seven sorrows, but many more beyond your recognition. It is a great feast in her name, but is also your feast! (Sept. 15 is the feast of the Mother of Sorrows).

My mother has lived the sorrows you bear and, because of this, you should always call on her in your time of need.

She is your mother and patron, who shall comfort you during your sorrow.

She is noted as your Mother of Sorrow for the seven sorrows she lived, but, I tell you, she is most powerful as your Mother of Sorrows, because she has experienced your sorrows.

In your sorrow you are bonded to her Immaculate Heart, and her tears for your sorrow purify you.

I tell you, the sword that pierces your hearts has pierced My mother's heart before your sorrow was betrothed to you!

When you call on her, she flies to your protection and cradles your heart! Allow her to comfort you for, when you are sorrowful, My mother is also. Allow her to unite your heart, to her Immaculate Heart.

The sword may pierce your heart, but the edge has been dulled, because it first pierced My mother's heart before your own.

Call on her. She shares your sorrow!

1

WORTHINESS

SEPTEMBER 20, 1989

My child, I speak to My people, not because of their holiness or worthiness, but because of My holiness and worthiness!

It is written in Scripture that the Son of Man shall save His people through His blood, and that His people shall be redeemed in Him.

KNOW THAT I COME TO MY PEOPLE, AND SPEAK TO THEM, TO FULFILL THE PROCLAMATION AS IT IS WRITTEN!

I AM THE SON OF GOD, YOUR LORD, JESUS CHRIST, FULFILLING THE WORTHINESS GIVEN TO ME FROM MY FATHER.

I AM YOUR LORD GOD, HERE TO SAVE YOU THROUGH MY HOLINESS!

I am here because of My worthiness in the Father, not because of your worthiness. It is through My blood that your redemption became possible. It is through My blood that I am consecrated to you and you to Me. The crucifixion was your redemption.

I wish to make it known to My people that I am here because it is written, in fulfillment of Scripture, that the Son of Man comes because of His holiness, and not because of your worthiness. Therefore, humble yourselves unto Me. Humbly accept My love and My teachings. Through them, you shall be able to humble yourselves to My Father, your Father of Mercy.

KNOW THIS IS TRUE. ALL SHALL BE FULFILLED IN ACCORDANCE TO THE WORD OF GOD.

LIVE IN THE PRESENT

SEPTEMBER 22, 1989

My people do not live for the present day. Their worries and anxieties stem from their anticipation of what tomorrow shall bring. In worrying about tomorrow, they have not lived for today.

I AM JESUS OF TODAY AND TOMORROW, AS I WAS YOUR JESUS YESTERDAY!

If you wish Me to be yours tomorrow, then have Me today! Focus on the moment, and on My great love. If you focus on tomorrow, tomorrow may not come! How can I fill you with My goodness and grant you My graces tomorrow if you will not accept them today?

Live for today in Me, My people.

Live in Me this very moment.

Structure your attention, and be focused on Me, this moment and every moment of each day.

. Live the graces I grant you each day by accepting them and taking one day at a time.

Do not run ahead! Do not look back!

Live the moment, and be aware of all the beauty I give to you.

Focus your energy on Me in everything you do.

You will be able then to accept My peace, because you will be walking with Me.

Do not worry what yesterday has brought, because today will become yesterday!

I tell you, My child, it is on rare occasions that My people live each day as if it were their last. My people plan for an uncertain future. I would like My people to return to basic principles. It is very difficult for My people, because of the world they created: a world of life against a time table; a world of fallacy, not reality; a world of competition, not unity; a world of struggle, not companionship; a world destined to hate from the lack of love and compassion. Is this a merciful path of life?

Take seriously My words, My beloved people, because My seriousness stems from My concern and love for you.

Many will say, child, that it is because of the condition of the world, and your desire to see it change, which has deceived you to think that I speak to you. They will not take My words seriously, and they will think that My words are really your own! I tell you, My heart saddens for these, My skeptics.

When the time comes in which they will know that these words are Mine, and the time will come, it shall be too late, for these words come through My Father.

I am asking My people in this lesson to live for today. Live day by day and focus on Me. Live in Me today, and you shall live in Me tomorrow!

Seek tomorrow without having found Me today and you shall not find Me, for the day of tomorrow is uncertain!

I tell you, child, this will be difficult for My people. I will see, now, how many of My people who say they trust in Me, really trust in Me! Can they live for today without anticipating tomorrow? Can they totally trust in Me today, that they will not worry about tomorrow? Will they be at peace with what I bring them today? Do My people truly trust in Me?

WISDOM

SEPTEMBER 25, 1989

My dear child, the mind is the source of all conduct.

The word spoken from the tongue results in the action of your deeds, your thoughts, the route to your words and actions. The man who seeks My Wisdom, and finds it, will reflect it through his thoughts, words and actions!

What does My Wisdom tell you? Wisdom in Me will teach you not to seek acceptance from man but to seek acceptance from My Father. My Wisdom teaches you not to put your trust in the human heart, for the human heart will torture you!

Trust in My Father. Trust in Him and you will find His goodness. Do not put your trust in man, but in God. Man stands by you in your time of joy, but only watches on in your time of sorrow. My Wisdom teaches you not to seek the words of praise from man, for those who speak words of praise, speak also words which are harmful and full of deceit. Man's words are words of no value!

Words of praise are words of nothingness, and harmful words

are words of no meaning. Put your trust in My Father, for the words of man are full of judgment. My Wisdom teaches you not to sway like thin branches on a tree. Be strong in your faith and firm in your trust in Him Who sent Me.

If you live in My peace, harmful words will not bother you, and words of praise will not move you to boast in pride. This is what My Wisdom teaches: for all to seek peace, praise and discipline from My Father, through trust and open-heartedness.

If you live in My Wisdom, I will teach you that the love of money deceives you and is the source of evil. If you love money, you love your prestige!

Take heed of My words on Wisdom. Happy the man who seeks My Wisdom, and finds it, for he shall live in joy. Happy the man who shares My Wisdom through his actions to his fellow companions. All mankind shall praise him, for they will be praising Me as I live in him!

TEMPERANCE

SEPTEMBER 29, 1989

My child, My people need to be cautious of what they put into their bodies. Be careful of how you feed your appetite. Do not overindulge, for the food you eat may kill you! Treat your body as a temple of God. Remain pure and be tender with your body. Be wise in your selections. Do not overeat and do not overdrink! Overdrinking leads to debauchery and beligerance!

My people are not aware how food will harm them. Eat to survive, and maintain your nutritional requirements. Overindulgence is foolish and will lead to suffering.

Drink your wine in moderation only, for you do not know when the Son of God shall come through the heavens. On that day, be careful to be sober and righteous in Me! What food you have in abundance, share with your brothers. Give to those who do not have. Do not keep your overabundance to yourself. SHARE!

After you have received your satisfactory nutritional assessment, give to those who have none and need to feed their appetite.

These are My words to you on temperance of your food. Nourish your soul with the food of everlasting life. You feed your bodies without feeding your souls. **It is your soul that lives and your bodies which die and return to dust!** Nourish your souls and do not worry about what food you shall eat to feed your appetites! Eat for nourishment, and not for overindulgence. Do not be gluttons!

SPIRITUAL HEALING

SEPTEMBER 30, 1989

My dear child, it is not physical healing which is the greatest gift from My Father, but the spiritual healing of the many lost souls.

I, your Jesus, continue healing My people's souls so that they can live forever.

The Son of Man came to gather His people and heal them spiritually. This was the main purpose I healed physical ailments...because of My Mother, Who suffered by seeing her children suffer through their diseases!

Know this, it is your souls which must be healed in order to receive everlasting life, not your bodies! I tell you, better for your bodies to be chastised now, than for your souls to be chastised later!

Allow Me to spiritually heal you, My people. This grace is the most vital. A nourished soul is a healthy soul. Healthy souls live!

Deceit is what I wish to cleanse and remove from your inner beings. I have mercy on your souls, and they rejoice in Me! I feed your souls with My Spirit and dwell in them at all times.

Come to Me, you in spiritual need! I shall give to you the

greatest gift from My Father. The physician need not heal the healthy, but the suffering.

I am here to heal you and mend your souls. I am here to restore them to health. I bring you hope, for if My Father did not allow Me to heal your soul spiritually, what a gloomy future of death would be ahead!

Pray for your spiritual health and seek My Father's kingdom.

I shall cast out the spirits in your souls, and infuse My Spirit of life and nourishment.

COMPLACENCY

OCTOBER 1, 1989

My child, My people do not listen to My prophets. If they do not believe what My select prophets say, they will not believe in My truth.

My people ask for signs. When I send signs, they do not believe! When I speak to My children of My desire, they do not believe. They listen to what is spoken in Scripture through the prophets I selected many ages ago, but will not listen or believe in My prophets of this age! It was the same for My prophets of the time before! They were not believed either, as today.

My people are living now, amongst My prophets of My Divine Age of Mercy, and they continue to react as if My chosen have nothing of value to speak! Those who do not believe in My prophets and disciples later say, "Lord, why did you not tell me these were your prophets? I would have believed them." I shall say to them, "If you did not believe in the ones I sent you, you would not have believed Me, for I lived in them!"

I tell you this, My child, because of the attitudes of nonchalance and uncaring. My people are harming one another. Too many of My people visualize Me as a distant God, and many do not even care if I am in the midst of their presence.

How would you like it, child, if you went to a gathering, and no one recognized your presence or cared if you were amongst them? How would you have Me respond?

I am waiting for My people at all times. My people need the support and love of one another, and the uncaring attitudes are destroying all hope for My love to exist.

Do not My people realize what they are doing to one another and themselves through their complacent attitudes? If My people recognized this truth, why do they not ask Me to change their hearts?

What does it take for My people to believe in Me, by believing in those I have sent, My prophets and disciples?

This is My pain: seeing the beauty of My people being destroyed through their lack of love.

THE COMPLACENT ATTITUDE *(cont'd.)*

OCTOBER 4, 1989

My people are so satisfied with themselves that their attitudes reflect no need for change. They do not wish for My Divine assistance to mold their hearts into the perfection of My goodness. Their attitudes do not seek to reflect the need for purification and, therefore, this results in the lack of growth.

My people speak of the need to reach out and support one another, but their attitudes and actions do not reflect their words. That is because of their complacent attitude. There are so few in number who allow Me to mold them into the true people I have created.

The lives of My people have been so influenced by the way of the world that the true person in character and beauty is masked by a falsified persona. As My people continue day by day in their complacency, they continue to live in a fake world of no reality! They continue to think that they know who they are, and their attitudes reflect the need for little assistance. They live in a tunnel of darkness with their happiness being superficial and only on the surface. The words

I tell you will sadden you, child, when I tell you that My people do not even realize this truth.

Complacency is an addiction of masking My truth through the attitude! My people have lived in this way so long that they do not even know that their way of life through their attitude is not a reality!

If I asked My people: "Do you know the real you? Or, who are you?" they would not be able to respond truthfully, because they have lived with a complacent attitude all their lives and they know of nothing else. They would become confused and would think they were losing their minds if I tried to change them by showing many truths about themselves without their allowing Me. They are so self satisfied that any suggestion for the need to look at their inner being would be bounced out as an inner conflict and loss of peace (which they actually create for themselves by their outlook and separation from My truth!)

This is complacency: an addiction to a self satisfaction attitude, masking the truth by living in a world of fallacy, and not knowing the true individual I have created!

My truth and My love challenges the complacent heart, and will conflict with the inner being until My Spirit rests in you through your acceptance of molding you to My perfection, the perfection of light and happiness.

Once My Spirit lives in the complacent heart, it takes you out of the tunnel of darkness into the pasture of freshness, and will journey with you forever!

DISHONESTY

OCTOBER 9, 1989

My child, in this next lesson I wish to speak to you, and My people dear to Me, about dishonesty.

If My people are dishonest with their wealth, how are they going to be able to handle the wealth I have promised them?

People live in this world placing so much value on money

and materialism that they allow it to control them. They become dishonest and not trustworthy.

How many times My people do not stand behind the principles of truth because of money. Money is their god, and dishonesty and lack of trust-worthiness are their fruitless rewards. If they cannot be honest with their earthly wealth, how will they receive My wealth graciously, humbly and with honesty? How, My child? They cannot now, and will not be able later, because they live in a world where they have made money all their life!

I tell you, money is not the source of life!

Can money save their souls?

Will money be their god in the life to come?

I AM THE SOURCE OF LIFE AND I PROVIDE THE SOURCE OF TRUE WEALTH!

But, even My people will not acknowledge their dishonesty! They will not ask for forgiveness, and allow Me to fill them with My honesty and make them trustworthy to receive My wealth! How narrow minded, self-centered and so dishonest My people have become. My people say they need money to live.

I say they need My Spirit of everlasting life to live!

They need money to feed them, not to control them. What they have ample supply of, should be shared with those who have none to fill their hunger. My people have allowed money to corrupt them with dishonesty. They are not even honest with themselves. Of the money they have, they say it is not enough! The richest of the rich in this mortal world are deceived through their dishonesty to believe they do not have enough.

Coupled with dishonesty, only a few will believe the truth of My words! There won't be many who believe that I have chosen you to come to and speak to! Why? Because My words are far too simple for their complex mentality!

"Jesus is all knowing with great intellect, and could not or would not speak simply." What poor souls roam your corrupt world!

My people, look at your inner being and see your dishonesty! Be honest with yourselves, and seek My trustworthiness by seeking My wealth. Those of you, who look at yourselves and see no stain because of your complacency, beware! It is you, who live in darkness.

My child, if only My people really believed in the wealth which awaits them in My Kingdom!
If only they could accept it by accepting Me!
If only they would allow Me to give them My wealth!
How rich they would truly be!

Thank you for writing My words.

GRIEF

OCTOBER 12, 1989

My people grieve over their current situations, yet they do not grieve over their souls. Their focal point, once again, is placed on the wrong subject.

I do not wish for My people to grieve, but they do not listen. They are so consumed with their problems that only confusion exists, which leads to additional grief.

I tell you, as I wish to tell My people, when someone is grieving, do not take on the burden and also grieve with them or for them! Pray for their peace and be compassionate. Support them spiritually and morally, but do not take on their grief. Be concerned and attentive to the status of your own soul, and never loose your focus from My Father. Love Him in good times and in bad times!

Sadly, many of My people must experience grief before they will surrender unto Me! If I did not love their souls and them, dearly, I would not care for them and would allow them to fall.

Remember, I, your Lord, know man's heart and know exactly what each soul requires to obtain ultimate bliss.

Many of My righteous people grieve from the effects that man creates and infringes upon them. Unfortunately, again, they grieve for the effects man has caused. They lose their focal point. My point of this lesson is to awaken those who grieve.

Do not grieve for an event that happens in your life, or your focus is no longer on Me! Will not your Lord, God, care for you? Do you trust in Me? If you wish to grieve, then grieve for the condition of your souls, but not for what your fellow brethren has caused!

BE GRATEFUL, MY PEOPLE, THAT MY FATHER IS FORGIVING.

BE GRATEFUL THAT JUDGMENT IS NOT BASED ON MAN'S STANDARDS.

BE GRATEFUL THAT HE HAS ALLOWED ME TO SAVE YOU.

BE GRATEFUL FOR HIS EVERLASTING MERCY.

DO NOT GRIEVE. REJOICE!

Take each day as I have prepared it for you.

Do not allow your vivid and vain imaginations to cause you grief.

Live in Me in each moment.

Do not run ahead.

Offer to Me your hearts and souls daily, and you shall be recompensed.

I shall give you the strength to carry on, but do not grieve for what man has done.

Focus on your souls and My Father's great love for you!

CO-REDEEMERS

OCTOBER 15, 1989

My child, I would like to begin by stating that there is no relation between time and the Eternal God!

GOD, WHO MADE THE WORLD THEN, HAS THE SAME WORD NOW! HE IS ETERNAL AS I AM ETERNAL, AND THE SOULS HE CREATED ARE ETERNAL! THE RELATION BE-TWEEN GOD AND SOULS IS ETERNAL! THAT WHICH GAVE RISE TO PUNISHMENT THEN, GIVES RISE TO THE SAME PUNISHMENT NOW!

THE PRECEPTS THEN ARE THE SAME PRECEPTS OF HIS LAW NOW. THESE PRECEPTS ARE STILL NOT PRACTICED. WHAT IS PRACTICED IS MERELY WORDS. THE PRECEPTS OF THE LAW FROM THE HEART ARE NOT PRACTICED.

GOD DOES NOT CHANGE, MAN CHANGES! HE IS, AND ALWAYS WILL BE, THE SAME GOD OF YESTERDAY, TODAY AND TOMORROW. MAN, CREATED BY HIM, IS FREE. I HAVE COME TO MAKE MAN MORE FREE!

However, if man chooses to walk away from Me for welfare and his own righteousness, he may do so freely. I will not hold him back. He may have his temporary life and welfare! I come to give man far more freedom and the graces of peace, happiness and wealth, freedom from all religions in which the oppressive causes are suffocating the true word of God!

My people do not realize it is dignity at its highest level I bring to them. I have announced this so that they may know that they are co-redeemers in Me through this dignity.

The angels, although perfect, are inferior to man. Inferior, because they do not have the power, as man, to sacrifice themselves in Christ for the redemption of man! My Father does not ask the angels to suffer and be imitators in Christ! It is man, who is invited to be a co-redeemer and imitator of Me, and procreators of souls who enter Heaven! However, man cannot understand this. Is it much too superior a thought, man as co-redeemer?

Begin to receive My dignity I wish to give you by allowing Me to give you pure hearts. The purer you are, the more you will understand. Impurity causes a dense thickness like fog! Use your senses and, then, My passions! See things clearly and with purity. Cleanse your minds by what your eyes give sight to! Be honest, pure, peaceful, merciful and sober, and your heart shall be pure and clear.

The evil one shall always attempt to snatch souls with his poison. Know that where I am, so is he, lingering. Where I evangelize, he will always try to prove Me wrong!

I will always protect My people from his weapon and external harm, but they must, interiorly, have the will to follow

Me, and be purified from his poisonous venom. Be co-redeemers in Me, My people. Receive My dignity by being imitators and procreators of My Father. It is good, and it is the power you have, that no evil can strip from you. Use your gifts of power, will, and goodness and peace!

Peace and goodness shall be yours!

ADDITIONAL LESSON—SIN

OCTOBER 18, 1989

This lesson shall be on sin: How you commit sin; what to do about sin committed, and how to prevent sin from staining your soul.

Sin is an act committed, either by thought or action, which paralyzes the soul of spiritual drink. It becomes a passion in thought or action, and drains the soul of many graces. You commit sin by allowing your mind or your body to control you through a disgraceful passion of evil.

When you receive a thought, your mind processes that thought which may funnel into one of two channels, the channel of good or the channel of evil. If you control your thoughts to reflect My goodness, by allowing My goodness, by allowing Me to assist you, then that thought will proceed to flow through the channel of goodness and follow through in your bodily actions. If you allow your thoughts to carry out in your bodily functions without allowing Me to dwell in you, you block My Spirit of Goodness and it will funnel down the channel of evil.

Since man is free, he has the choice of good and evil. That is why the two exist! If you dwell on evil, evil will possess you, but if you dwell on Me and My goodness, it is sure to protect you and teach you the way to eternal perfection!

When you sin, allow My Spirit to truthfully guide you to honest reconciliation, and your soul will be nourished. Once absolution of your sin is completed, you become virginal in purity. Prevent sin by trusting in Me. Trust in Me by allowing Me to dwell in you at all moments.

Since man is free, he has the freedom of choice at all moments to select good or evil. Once sin has been committed in vain, and I then dwell in you, My Spirit will cause conflict with the evil until reconciliation has commenced! THAT SIN WILL CONTINUOUSLY STAIN THE SOUL UNTIL YOU ALLOW FORGIVENESS FROM ME AND YOURSELF!

REMEMBER, I CANNOT FORGIVE YOU IF YOU HOLD BOUND YOUR SIN BY NOT FORGIVING YOURSELF!

The conflict and separation of inner being will exist until you allow My goodness to prevail. However, once I have entered your soul, the conflict cannot last long because no evil can exist very long when I possess the soul. It is as I have said before, water and oil cannot emulsify. There will always be a separation.

When you receive a thought, think good and I will be invited in you! If you sin, ask My Spirit for a truthful and honest cleansing. In order for this to happen, you must allow and accept the truth with openness, sincerity and honesty.

This is the truth on sin, child. Always stand guard against it through My shield of protection. TRUST IN YOUR JESUS EACH MOMENT OF EACH DAY.

Bless you, and My peace I give you.

FATIGUE

OCTOBER 21, 1989

My dear child, there are many of My people who, in their tiredness, pass off their ill manners and conceit as an excuse for their fatigue. Many say, "Not today, I am too tired," and allow bad feelings and thoughts to control their actions. There is a Judas in all of My people!

How many times Judas had the desire to follow My ways and learn My goodness, but fell because he was tired or he allowed his intellect to be superior to the truth of My words! He did not seek God first nor did he trust in the truth of My words. He used tiredness as a scapegoat against facing the truth. So it is with My people.

There is a little of Judas in everyone until they allow Me totally, at all times, to possess their souls with the truth of My Father. As I gave hope to Judas time after time, again I give all My people hope, for it will never be Me, Who defies them, but they, who defy Me! They have that choice. **They select in freedom what they truly desire for their heart's and soul's nourishment.**

I would like to tell My beloved ones not to use their fatigue as a scapegoat from constantly and consistently working on the truth I have been teaching! Instead, endorse (to give approval, support, sanction: Webster) yourself for a hard day's work and allow Me to live in you. I shall give you rest. This will make you strong and enrich the power of your faith.

Always be on guard and do not allow tiredness to express feelings of deceit. Constantly work for your soul's welfare. Even in your rest does your soul require drink from the well of fresh water! Always be on guard, My people! When you feel tired and irritable, call on Me and I shall flee to you. I will remove your feelings and instill the truth of My presence and peace.

TRUST, My people, trust in your Jesus.

I AM YOUR INTIMATE GOD, HERE FOR THE RESTORATION OF THE WORLD!

INTERNAL SUFFERING

OCTOBER 26, 1989

My dear people, do not allow the evil one to torment you interiorly and cause harm to your soul. Always call on My Mother and Me and We will flee to your aide. Do not allow undue duress, because the evil one wishes to see you unhappy and weeping. Know he does not want those who have turned to him, but he wants those closest to Me!

Always be cautious and stand firm in your faith. When you feel that you are alone, not loved and unimportant, you can be sure I am closest to you. This is a fact. When you are in need, interiorly, I give you My strength to persevere. I bleed for you from My wounds when you are under attack from the evil one. My blood is your salvation, and I joyfully suffer for you when you are suffering, for We are united in My Father's oneness!

You may not feel any different, or at peace in your suffering but, I assure you that this suffering, when offered to My Father for merciless sinners, is the most potent offering in penance.

YOU SUBMERGE YOURSELF INTO MY ABANDONMENT AND SALVATION RESULTS THROUGH MY MERCY! IT BRINGS ETERNAL GLORY TO YOUR SOULS.

Suffering interiorly is the most painful and the ultimate test of your faith in My Father's goodness. This is the most viable suffering, the suffering man cannot see with his eyes, only with his heart! It is union with Me, sharing My suffering for the salvation of merciless sinners.

THE PRESENCE OF JESUS

OCTOBER 28, 1989

My child, I do not wish for My people to be wounded interiorly. I wish for their souls to receive eternal glory.

I would like to tell My people that, when they are persecuted, wounded in spirit and wracked by hatred from enemies, I am persecuted and wounded for them and with them! When they are wounded by life in this mortal world, peace cannot find her resting place. It is a constant battle, the division in the struggle of life and the search for life hereafter.

I wish My people to know that I am with them through their mortal life and after. I weep with them and endure the brunt of their major pain for them. That is what life in the material world causes...pain.

I came as Son of Man to stir up division and separation so that all, who wished to dwell with Me, could do so. It is the same now! I am here to bring peace but, in order for peace to reign, there will be separation.

Man will go against man and the battle of evil and good will commence. The man of good shall break off from the men of evil. The men of evil judgment shall celebrate in the victory of battle but, I tell you, their celebration will be premature. Their celebration will result in their damnation and agony, as they scream in the fires of Gehenna. No, the troop of glory, the men of God, shall reign forever and win in victory for all eternity, and peace shall be their flag.

I tell you this so all may know of the peace to come! So all may know that, when they are wounded, I bleed for them. For each drop of blood shed, salvation results for their eternal glory. What seems to be a loss in battle results in eternal victory.

Tell My people not to be deceived to think they have been defeated. The power of God reigns now, and shall for eternity!

GOODNESS

OCTOBER 30, 1989

My dear child, it pleases Me to hear you speak of your knowledge of My Father's goodness. Your prayers have caused My Angels to sing and rejoice, and I wish for all My people to know your words because, tonight, I wish to speak of goodness. These were your sweet words learned from My teachings:

> "Jesus, have mercy on the wicked, for there is good in them. Your Father created them, and all He creates is good. They do not know their wickedness, be merciful and patient. Your goodness shall reign."

You do not know, child, the power you have been granted in your prayer. I hear every word you pray, and respond. I listen most heartedly to you for you listen in obedience to Me. Goodness, attainable to all My people, prevails through mercy. When you are merciful and loving, the goodness of My presence presides. The wicked ways of My people turn to good when they are loving and merciful! All wickedness ceases to exist in the presence of My goodness. If you are good, you will cease being wicked, because I dwell in you. Utilize your faith totally in Me and be comforted. Allow your faith in Me to comfort you through total trust. Lack of trust and confidence are major roadblocks for My people, who strive to progress in spiritual goodness.

Goodness is a grace, and it, along with faith, mercy and love, is a most powerful tool to obtain guaranteed salvation and eternal glory. Souls need My goodness; they thirst for it. Being kind and merciful will quench the thirst of your soul, and grant you the grace of My goodness.

When you are good, then miracles can happen! Miracles are a grace you obtain through your goodness. They are not granted to you because they are due, and cannot be taught! The grace only comes from being good, and living in My goodness. Remember, once you receive the grace in the eyes of God, you will receive miracles. Know, also, that souls are saved through kindness and mercy—My goodness, EVEN THOUGH THEY ARE DEEMED UNWORTHY THROUGH THE WICKEDNESS OF HUMANITY.

Goodness is the true facet of mercy and love through kindness, compassion and unquestionable faith in your living God.

THE LIVING GOD

NOVEMBER 1, 1989

I wish My people to perceive Me as a living God, and accept My Spirit as the source of all goodness. My people do not perceive Me as living as they live! They do not will My presence to live in them. What their minds cannot conceive intellectually, they cannot understand nor accept.

Even as I tell you I live in the true sense of the word, their thoughts cannot comprehend it because they do not accept this truth. Many can feel My Spirit in them but they do not believe that I am I, in the truest sense, living in them, with them! My people think that God, being the higher authority, created them but that they cannot be like Him. This is not true!

God created man in the likeness and image of Me, so that all could live in oneness with the Trinity.

Man does not seek perfection in the eyes of God. He belittles himself! All men should seek the kingdom of God, knowing that the kingdom belongs to them, and was created so that they could have eternal glory through Me. I wish for all My people to know, that in their imperfection of humanity, they are made perfect in the eyes of God, should they seek it in all goodness.

How My people restrict themselves by limiting, with their minds and hearts, what is attainable. **What man does not understand with his mind, he does not seek!** If man does not understand God, he will not seek Him! That is why I always spoke in parables.

Man could not understand the truth of My words, and would only accept what he wanted to hear, had I not spoken in parables. Even now, in these lessons, few will grasp the total truth and seek My Father's Kingdom.

Today, I wish for My people to know My Father, Who lives with their hearts and their thoughts. He will grant you strength to persevere, and wisdom in His eyes. He will comfort you, not harm you! He will cradle you like a newborn babe. He will not enslave you, but give you everlasting freedom, which your souls desire and plead.

KNOW YOUR GOD. HE IS YOUR FRIEND FOR ALL ETERNITY! CALL HIM ABBA, FOR HE IS YOUR 'DADDY'! HE IS MY ABBA, AND HE IS YOUR ABBA!

REJOICE, O HIGHLY FAVORITE ONES, YOU ARE THE NEW ISRAEL, WHERE ONLY PEACE, LOVE AND FREEDOM SHALL BE HER FRUITFUL GIFTS! ALL WHO SEEK THE KINGDOM, THE KINGDOM OF GOD, SHALL ENTER AND LIVE FOR ALL ETERNITY!

ATTENTION TO CHOSEN

NOVEMBER 4, 1989

My people, please be attentive to My apostles of this century! Take heed of their words, for their words are My words. There is not much time left for salvation. Use every minute you have to prepare your soul for My Father's judgment. DO NOT WASTE ANY TIME!

The time you have has been granted as a grace period to assist you in your conversion. I do not speak, this day, of comfort. I plead with you for your obedience and attentiveness to My apostles. I speak for a purpose.

If you choose to be with Me, safe in eternal glory, then take heed of My words through My chosen! I have assigned My watchman, who knows My hour. Correct your evil ways! The soul cannot survive without My love.

If you think it can or do not believe in your soul's journey, then, so be it, and walk the path of darkness and doom! If you question the truth, and wonder if I truly speak to My apostle, then, I tell you, better to believe than not! For the hour I come, you must be prepared! I will take those, whom I find ready and waiting with hope, to dwell with Me.

MAKE NO MISTAKE. THIS IS NOT ILLUSION. THIS IS FACT. PREPARE, AND TURN TO YOUR GOD.

HE AWAITS YOU TO SHOWER YOU WITH GOODNESS, JOY, PEACE AND ETERNAL COMFORT!

SORROW

NOVEMBER 7, 1989

My dear child, My people have sorrow because they are slaves to sin! If they would come to Me, I would purify and cleanse them. I would wash them with My blood, the blood of forgiveness. I do not call My people to Me to be slaves, but to be My Saints!

There are those, who come to Me out of curiosity, running busily here and there, but making no effort towards a true contrition. So they live in their sorrow. Oh! If My beloved would come to receive Me in My Eucharist, I would cleanse them and comfort them. I would place the truth of My law in their hearts and on their minds. The sorrow is that they cannot accept the truth of My words, and do not believe that My sacrifice for men was to sanctify them through forgiveness in My bloodshed.

I CAME TO DO THE WILL OF GOD, HIS WILL OF SAVING MAN FROM CONDEMNATION AND SANCTIFYING THEM THROUGH MY BLOOD FOR REDEMPTION.

My sorrow is viewing the many who do not wish to receive My Body and Blood. **If only one priest performed consecration of My Eucharist in only one sanctuary, people would flock to receive Me. They would want to see the Divine Mysteries.** But there are many priests who have the power of My Mystery and, yet, there are so few who receive it with an open heart!

My people live in sorrow, a pain deeply embedded in their souls. As each day goes by, their pain does not alleviate, but continues to deepen until their hearts turn cold, and then to ice! The numbness exists and they co-exist, not as co-redeemers, but as co-destructors! They exist in the only possible way. . .with no love! Their sorrow and pain are true, which clouds their hearts, minds and souls with such viscosity that they mourn. The mourn because their souls thirst for love and honesty, but their hearts have turned to ice! If only they would come to Me, I would refresh them with life, the love of life and the beauty of all creation.

Man will not be able to exist much longer with icy hearts because the soul will die. Love, and openness to receive love through the heart, nourishes the soul. If you do not wish My love and gifts, your hearts will freeze and your souls die! Do not allow the glamour of evil to hypnotize you. Evil will mesmerize you, then deceive you! Your oxygen of life will be depleted and your hearts will grow cold until final damnation freezes them, and the soul mourns in death for all eternity.

Come to Me, My dear people of My creation. Allow Me to refresh you and replenish you with life. Come to Me and

I shall give you plentiful drink, the true nourishment and soul's requirement for life, comfort, happiness and peace. Come to Me and receive My mercy, the gift of your redemption which awaits to be claimed.

HOLY SPIRIT

NOVEMBER 27, 1989

Who is the Holy Spirit? What does the Holy Spirit mean to you? How can you acquire the living presence of My Spirit at all times? These are questions My dear people need so badly to have answered, and digest!

My people continue to die a slow death! They die from their own poison, the poison of judgment, spite, resentfulness, envy, hatred, fear and their own control, the strong poisonous venom of the soul! If My people invited My Spirit to be their spouse, their poison would turn into their cure.

Who is the Holy Spirit?

The Holy Spirit is My Divine Spirit, Who literally dwells in your physical, bodily formation as your spirit. He is united to the spirit of the soul and body to become a living, walking Spirit of My Father. When the Spirit exists and dwells in you, you share in My life in all phases and in all totality.

From the human conception, My people should perceive the Holy Spirit as a living person. It is like a blind person, who cannot see another living person, but knows with his mind and heart that there are people living in bodily form. My Spirit is a living person, Who unites His Spirit to your existing spirit, and grants gifts of salvation, peace, beauty and endless graces.

SEE MY SPIRIT AS A BLIND PERSON SEES YOU!
THE SPIRIT IS ALIVE.
THE SPIRIT IS A PERSON.
THE HOLY SPIRIT IS YOUR PROTECTION.
THE HOLY SPIRIT IS YOUR DIVINE SPOUSE OF LOVE!
NEVER, NEVER FORGET THIS! NEVER!

The moment you forget is the moment you have lost your desire for eternal life. The Holy Spirit means life! He is the truth of My life. He unites the soul to the Holy Trinity. He will speak to you. HE WILL SPEAK!

Do you not speak to a blind man? Listen, and acutely utilize your senses! The Holy Spirit means protection and endless happiness. He is your spouse, your brother, your father, your most intimate friend. All comforts come through Him, all blessings, discernment and knowledge! That is what the Spirit means to you.

THE HOLY SPIRIT IS YOUR SALVATION! INVITE MY SPIRIT! That is how you acquire My presence. . .simply ASK! Then listen and trust.

Once the Spirit is dwelling in you, if you do not trust in Me, you do not trust in yourself! For, once My Spirit enters, you are consecrated to the Divine Holy Trinity. If you do not trust Me, you do not trust My Spirit in you and you cannot trust yourself. If a blind man does not trust you, he cannot trust himself, because he would live in fear of deceit and harm! You must trust in My Spirit as I trust in you. There will commence comfort and the oh-so-many gifts which await you.

Tell My people, child, tell them! MY SPIRIT AWAITS TO MAKE THE BLIND MAN SEE!

PRAYER

NOVEMBER 28, 1989

My dear child, I wish for all My people to pray with universal intentions. It is much more powerful when you pray for a quantity of people instead of one person at a time. If you wish one person to be healed, then pray for all the people who need to be healed. The power of prayer is so intense that, the more people you pray for universally, the greater healings are granted! The stronger the forces of good prevail on your behalf.

The angels await My people's prayers so that they may proclaim them in song to My Father! Make no mistake about prayer. It must be made known to My people that universal prayer, in its entirety, is the spark to igniting a chain of healing graces. Tell My people not to pray only for themselves or their families. Pray for all! Pray for world conversion, world peace, My priests and sisters. Pray for the unemployed, the homeless, the sick. Pray for the dying and especially those souls in Purgatory. They await your prayers.

Tell My people to pray! Tell them of the power they have been granted through Me in loving prayer. I say loving prayer, for any unloving prayer will be struck down and return to the soul from which it derived to cause grief.

This lesson on prayer is not a personal one, child, it is for all My people, for when I speak to you, I am speaking to them. Let them know that you are My child of the world! As St. Peter symbolizes the father of this world of all people and generations, you are Our child of all the generations, the symbol of children. For all, who are children, shall enter the Kingdom of God.

Tell My people to pray with the innocence and purity of children. Tell them of their power. A childlike prayer penetrates to the core of My Father's throne. All are children of God. It is necessary to use My graces through innocent prayer.

SALVATION OF SOULS

NOVEMBER 29, 1989

There are three phases to the salvation of souls!

The first phase is that of truth and honesty. The soul is wounded in grief. It is speaking without fear and acceptance. The soul bleeds because it does not wish to be wounded and the speaker grieves; also, because he does not wish to wound. SOULS THAT NEED SALVATION MUST FIRST BE WOUNDED TO ACCEPT THE TRUTH THAT THEY ARE IN DANGER. It is like waves in the sea which circulate until they crash on solid land!

Secondly, after acceptance, the soul wishes to silently repent. It will weep and dare to approach an apostle with open heartedness and honesty. The healing of these souls comes from the charity of God!

Those, who are apostles of God, only find charitable words of comfort and love. It is the sweet honey which coats the soul's grievous and painful wounds.

Thirdly, the soul does not live in fear! It is bold and goes on a mission where one would normally flee. It knows the protection of God, and it rejoices in ecstatic gratitude to fertilize the seeds planted in other souls. It crushes the fermented wickedness from evil and replaces noncombustable love!

I tell you this, child, so My people will not sulk in their grief when. they are spiritually wounded. The existing soul must first be wounded so that it can be nurtured and strengthened with true purity. Tell My people to bear their weaknesses for I, their Saviour, will give them strength, and bring them to My green pastures.

THE SOUL LIVES AND PREPARES ON EARTH ONLY TO CONTINUE LIVING IN MY KINGDOM OF PEACE AND SERENITY. It is meritorious when the soul is wounded for it is its salvation! Tell them not to be afraid. I am with all My people. EACH ONE BELONGS TO THE SHEPHERD, WHO HAS COME TO GATHER HIS WOUNDED SHEEP!

SAINTHOOD

DECEMBER 4, 1989

Today My people live in a world of fallacy. I wish for all My people to be My saints, but My people do not fully understand what a saint is!

A saint is one who has no personal desire, but wishes to fulfill the desires of all people's hearts through My goodness. Anyone who desires worldly goods and spiritual freedom can never be a saint!

Those who act saintly are not necessarily a saint! To be

a saint, you must be one from within! If you act as a saint
on the surface only, you deprive yourself and others of the
treasures of life. Remember, also, that to be a saint does not
mean that man will not find error in you. What constitutes
sainthood today, from your measures, is not what constitutes
sainthood from the standards of My Father.

I want My people to know that all are invited to be saints
on earth and in Heaven! Look to Us and We will prepare
you, mold you and guide you. I wish, also, to remind My
people that their world has turned into a world of hatred among
brethren. If they feel that recognition from a man is necessary
to be a saint, they are wrong.

There is little recognition today because of little love, but,
if all remember to seek acceptance from Me, then they would
not need any recognition from the world, because I would
fill them with an overabundance of love. They would want
to give love, instead of receive it. I tell you, My beloved spouse,
there are few people, today, who seriously have the desire
to be Our saints.

It is My hope, with this lesson, that all My chosen will
recognize My call for them to be true, real saints, inwardly
and externally! It is a call, not to act saintly, but to be authen-
tic! It is possible!

My hope in My people is that they will hear My words
with their hearts and ask Me! All they need do is ask. Those
who choose to ridicule and slander the words I have spoken
to each heart, and choose recognition through worldly props,
such as money, choose to walk with satanism. There are many
empty seats on My throne because many of My people have
not believed that I extended an invitation to them to be My
saints. There are now still available spaces for saints to come,
if My people believe sainthood is attainable through humility
and lack of pride! **It is not their humanness I want, My
child, it is their souls.**

Sainthood awaits all who desire it, and reflect their love
for My Father through genuine humbleness and elimination
of self pride! The way to this journey is to simply ask without
ambivalence. I shall mold them according to the soul!

KNOW AND ACCEPT, DO NOT FEAR

DECEMBER 6, 1989

My dear child, those who walk in the truth of My light will accept the truth of themselves in their journey of growth. Be grateful that man is not judged by man, but by My Father! He is the judge of all men and He is a gracious, patient and loving God.

Each day, as My people choose to be closer and closer to Me, they will come to know themselves and accept themselves with love. The ego slowly dwindles away and disintegrates, and My people will even accept and acknowledge their human faults. Then they will no longer walk in false humility but be the budding beauties of humbleness!

Each day, as My people elect to accept My truth and My love, they will no longer attack themselves, because they make or have made errors, but, will also embrace My love as their salvation! My people will know with all of their hearts, minds and souls that, even though they try and fail, they have won in My sight!

I am not looking for perfectionism, but genuine sensitivity.

I desire their hearts to be filled with honesty and purity.

Remember, I see the deepest incentives of each person's heart.

Conversion, although a journey in time, is also simple. It is man who complicates and makes conversion a word of struggle! That is why those, whose hearts belong to Me, suffer. They suffer a longing for peace and love between mankind, but live with the reality of deceit and sorrow! These are My pure children, for only I know their suffering, which is not shared with mankind. No one sees their suffering, only the Holy Trinity.

I WANT MY PEOPLE TO KNOW NOT TO FEAR! Those who fear or instill fear, live with imperfect love. I have said, and shall say again, that I will save My people.

I WILL NOT ALLOW ONE OF MY CHOSEN TO BE HARMED! All shall have eternal freedom. Do not be afraid of what may come ahead. All those who wish to be Mine shall be saved, for all who desire shall be called my chosen!

Fear has no substance! What justice is there in fear? If you fear, do you have faith in Me? My people, do not be afraid. The power of God, My Father, is so intense in fortitude that, if He wanted to destroy everything and everyone, it would only take a matter of a second in terms of your time! My Father is a loving Father and He loves you. So do not be fearful of what may come, but be grateful that He loves you and cares so much for you that all, who wish to be His, will be! It is that simple. Ask and allow Us to purify you.

My Father and I are dedicated to you in granting eternal salvation and freedom! If you do not desire Us, as We desire you, then so be it! It is your choice, and shall always be your choice, not Ours. Our wish is to protect you and grant you the pleasing comfort of serenity and peace. Those of you, who think that Jesus would not speak in so pedestrian a way, know that you live in a complex world, because you have allowed complexity of your intellect to control you.

I speak simple words so that there will be no mistake or misunderstanding of My offer of everlasting life to you. I speak clearly and directly to ALL created by My Father, and so that all will understand. There is no favoritism in the Kingdom of God. All share in and live in the oneness of My Father's love.

CONVERSION

DECEMBER 10, 1989

My dear child, humanity remonstrates, also, in good, simple people. I have taken them away from their families, their businesses, and their social affairs. This remonstration, internal protest, shall be calmed because My good will come to see My light. It is difficult, at first, to walk with your Jesus because I take you through the fog, the mud, to green pastures. My people have difficulty, at first, because they think that their walk with Me will be as they have it mapped out in their minds. Then they come to know their true Jesus.

I tell you, they will rejoice after their journey of conversion, that I have taken them through the fog and mud, and they will understand this is conversion! It is like a dandelion. As the wind blows, the dangelion tufts are released. Many float in the air and many land on My lap! The tufts are My disciples. My floaters are those who wander, and those who land on My lap may float away too, due to fear, frivolity, inconstancy, selfishness, pride and even foolishness! I wonder how many disciples will truly come to Me in the most crucial moments of My mission!

There are few who rest on My lap presently, and I pray for those floating tufts to land on My lap. I also pray for those who have landed in My care, that they are not blown away after the first gust of wind, for all have their will to choose until the last moment.

How My people struggle in their loyalty to Me. Pray for them, My child. Pray for all My tender tufts, My disciples, and bring them back home to Me!

FIDELITY

DECEMBER 13, 1989

My dear child, I, your dear Jesus, wish to speak today on fidelity. It was not through the law that Abraham and his descendants inherited the land. It was through their faith that what was promised to him would be delivered, and he would be able to accomplish all that he was told. If those who adhere to the law are heirs, then faith is null and the promise is void. Where there is no law, there also is no violation.

Fidelity is the strongest bond to the Divine, Holy Trinity through faithfulness. It is My righteous who become righteous in their faith! The law will never promise righteousness to you. Only through dedicated faith in My Father will all be deemed righteous; for this He has promised! It will be through fidelity that I shall unite My righteous. They will all be gathered under one Kingdom and that Kingdom will be Mine! There will no longer be nations and separate kingdoms. There will only be one, and this one Kingdom will last for all eternity in My peace.

It will be credited to those, who do not doubt My Kingdom, for they shall be empowered by My faith and shall give great glory to My Father. **Oh, then shall My people know that I am their Lord!**

How I shall reproduce the land and populate My children! All shall sing praises and be united in comfort and peace. Oh, how this fruitful season is now at hand and all, who live in Me through the powerful gift of fidelity, shall be the new lambs of God for all eternity! For nation shall rise against nation and kingdom against kingdom, but My Israel will stand united at the end as the only one nation, one Kingdom of peace.

My Israel is all My beloved people throughout this entire world who claim My Father's zeal of faith and love through My Divinity! That will be My new Israel and all are invited to live in the City of Hope, through their fidelity in My Father.

This now ends My third set of lessons to My people. It is today that I re-consecrate My heart to all who desire it, and make known My devoted protection and care for all.

Know My Kingdom will come! Whether it comes through peaceful means or as a result of destruction through hatred will depend on you, My people. Choose peace and peace shall come. Choose destruction and My Father will destroy all who destruct. Only peace and love will reign in the Kingdom. Destruction and hatred will cease.

So I give the selection to you, My people. Your destiny depends on your prayers and relies on your faith. The secret is fidelity, love, mercy, hope, trust and acceptance of My truth to result in a joyful and peaceful destiny.

I love you, My beloved people. PLEASE LOVE ME. How can I bring you peace unless you desire it? If you desire peace, would you not be merciful and loving to one another, to those people who belong to Me as you belong to Me? Are you not creating your own destiny? Select the path you wish to walk very carefully. For it is truly a matter of eternal life or eternal death!

GUARD AGAINST EVIL

DECEMBER 18, 1989

My child, tell My people to be on guard against the evil one and his followers. Where there is good, so too will evil be!

Live by the doctrine of My Church. All those who do not are not of Me, but from the evil one. Always look to Me for the truth you seek. I shall always protect all those who desire to reign with Me, for they who desire are My chosen ones.

If I say to you that I promise you eternal life and peace, then all I say will be fulfilled! Live in your faith. That what I speak will be granted. If you truly trusted in Me, then you would truly believe that what I say will be fulfilled in the glory of My Father. I am not here to enslave My people, but to free them!

I died for all so that all would live! I died for you so that your soul would never die. I am a God Who wishes for all to share in all My glory. All I have I give to you. There are no restrictions.

I do not wish for My people to feel guilty or have any feelings of remorse, because I love them and am a forgiving God. ALL THEY NEED TO DO IS COME TO ME AND FORGIVE THEMSELVES, SO THAT I CAN FORGIVE THEM.

It is a simple and true oath I have given to My people, yet, so hard for them to grasp. I promise everlasting life, and they have a difficult time believing that they shall have it. I tell them that I live, and they wonder! I speak to them, and they doubt in My truth. I tell them to be on guard for the evil one, and they shun Me away, afraid that I am he! If they would come to Me before My Blessed Sacrament, they would know that **I am their Jesus of Mercy** and all of which I speak will be fulfilled!

These are the many types of My people, child. Make note of them, for they are all good, yet lost. There are My people who do not feel worthy and are full of remorse, guilt and low self acceptance, knowing their merit alone would never gain their entrance into Heaven. There are those who are appre-

hensive and overly cautious. These people of Mine are con-
trolled by their intellect and rely little on their knowledge
given through their hearts. These are My doubting Thomases
who wonder if My lessons are truly from Me. Then there
are My confident people, My people of pride; those who make
their time table. But I am at the end of the list! They are
the ones who have little or no time for Me. They are en-
thralled with success and life and power. These are still My
people, whom only money has enticed to the point where
it becomes their god, My people of materialism!

I tell you about the different types of people, child, because
they all belong to Me. They all are good, but need the grace
of My salvation. Those people who do not belong to Me are
those who have given their soul to the evil one! They are
those who worship idols, and do not practice the doctrine
of My Church. They are forever gone because they choose
to walk with Satan! Those who fall into the trap of evil, can
be saved through prayer and devotion. However, those who
turn away by their own free will from the Trinity, lose life
forever!

So, I tell My people this day to be on guard against the
evil one, but to know that I am their Jesus of Truth and Faith.
I will protect all who come to Me, for all eternity!

I wish to tell My people of low self esteem and fears to
rejoice, for I shall release them from all enslaved feelings
of remorse. In their simpleness, they have been redeemed.
All I have promised them will take place. They shall gain
Heaven because I merit it for them. Do not worry about your
worthiness, for I, your Jesus, am worthy, and all who live
in Me shall gain eternal life through Me only, not through
your merits. And I have said I shall share everything with
all My people, so Heaven awaits you!

To My cautious and apprehensive ones, those of great intellect, seek Me with your heart. See Me from within and
live in My holiness! If you truly trusted in Me, you would
know Me and you would know with your heart and with your
mind that these lessons are from Me, your Jesus, and from
Me ONLY, for I am GOOD, I am PURE. There is no evil

in Me. If man can promise and speak to man of many things, can not God speak to His people and have fulfilled what is promised? Know what I say is true!

Come before My Blessed Sacrament and be intimate with Me. Know the gift of your intellect was given from My Father. Use it to know My truth, that it is truly your Jesus speaking! Do not allow the way of the world or evil to fog your intellect. Come before Me and you shall see clearly that My Father has allowed Me to speak to you. You will no longer be apprehensive.

And to My people who are on the edge of darkness, My people of pride and confidence, My people of success and money, I urge you to pray! Do not be deceived by your materialism. If you do not have time for My Father, make time or He will not have time for you in your hour of most need. If you are so sure that you do not need to pray as I have asked, or do not need Me, then be sure that you are in most need of My Divine Mercy!

It is you who are My lost ones. It is you for whom My heart bleeds. It is you who are the farthest away. If you give money in order to receive recognition, beware! Your only recognition will be from man. Do not allow money to be your god of power. There is only one God of power. Find Me before it is too late! I never said you must be poor to enter Heaven. I have only said you must not have a love for money, as your god. Do not be powerful through your money. Be powerful through Me. There is so much I wish to give to you. My treasures are of more value than the most money your mind can conceive. Humble yourselves so that you can be first. Live as you are now, and you shall be last, if at all!

THE LORD'S PRAYER

DECEMBER 22, 1989

My dear child, tonight I wish to speak to My people about the meaning of the most pure and perfected prayer, the prayer of My Father, your "Our Father." It is necessary that all know and understand the meaning of this prayer. The eloquence of the words are the ultimate of perfection, the perfection of His love.

I have told you and My people that all, who live in Me, live in My Father, for We are one as you and I are one in Him. ALL WHO COME TO ME ARE, IN TURN, DELIVERED TO HIM WHO HAS SENT ME. If you live in My faith, you live in Him, and the power of His love is your salvation.

The prayer of the "Our Father" is My prayer which was taught to all, so that all may share in His grace of perfection. If your prayer is that of Mine, then your prayer is one of perfection, and you are perfected in Me through Our oneness. It is the most beautiful prayer and the purest, the ultimate prayer of divine protection!

'Our Father Who art in Heaven': denotes the Father of all mankind, all races; the eternal and true, living God Who is your Father, dwelling in the place prepared for all His loved ones, the place of paradise and everlasting peace.

'Hallowed be Thy Name': glorious is His Name, for glory will be given to all who praise Him and share in His love.

'Thy Kingdom come': His kingdom of peace will reign for all eternity in His goodness.

'Thy will be done on earth as it is in Heaven': purity, truth, love, mercy, compassion, honesty, joy and peace will be on earth, for it is in His kingdom! Earth, created by Him in all His beauty, shall return to beauty and remain a paradise as His Kingdom. And truth, joy, charity, hope, compassion, humility, strength, faith, His love and mercy shall be His symbols.

'Give us this day our daily bread': feed our souls with Your nourishment to share in eternal glory.

'Forgive us our trespasses': forgive our selfishness and pride against Your beloved ones. Forgive us, for we have offended Your honor.

'As we forgive those who trespass against us': for we pray for reconciliation of our brothers who have offended our honor in Your name.

'Lead us not into temptation, but deliver us from evil': protect us from all harm, and keep us pure from sin caused by

the evil one, so that we may live in the oneness and purity
of the Divine Holy Trinity.

This, My dear one, is the true meaning of His prayer which
is My prayer and which is your prayer; the prayer of perfection and one which is hoped to be said with an open heart.
Tell My people to pray it, for it is His prayer, and simplicity
is its armor!

MOTHER OF ALL CHILDREN

DECEMBER 23, 1989

My dear little one, I wish for all of My beloved people
to know that as I came from the womb of My mother, so
did they! Not only was I nourished in her womb, but My
people were also nourished in her, for she is the 'Mother
Of All Children.'

If I say to you that you are perfected in Me and will share
in My glory, are you not perfected in My mother? She is
the mother of mankind, and We are one in each other. If
she shares in My glory, and I have said that My people will
share in My glory, are you not sharing in her glory? Are
you not from her womb, if you live in Me and I am of her
womb?

My people think that I, their God, am a distant and righteous God and that they are people of no degree of holiness,
only the slaves of the Holy One. This is not true. **I am your
God of Mercy. I am your God Who gives to you all that
I have. I am your God Who desires to be one with all,
as I am one with My Father and one with My mother.**

My mother is NOT slave to Me. My saints are NOT slaves
to Me. They are one with Me, and My kingdom is their kingdom! They reign with Me, and all I have is theirs. If I have
given to them all of what I have said, and I have said that
there is no favoritism, does that not mean that My kingdom
belongs also to you? There are no slaves in the kingdom. I
wish for all people to grasp this truth, and believe with all

their hearts that what I have is for them, not for Me!

They have difficulty because there is no king on earth who gives what belongs to him. What man gives without expecting something (even love may be an expectation, child) in return? They are afraid to be intimate with Me. I WANT MY PEOPLE TO COME TO ME AND TALK TO ME AS THEY WOULD AN INTIMATE FRIEND. I WANT TO BE THAT INTIMATE FRIEND!

Listen to Me, My child. There is so much hatred in your world that love is growing cold. I cannot even plead with My beloved people, because they have allowed this disease of hatred to spread throughout their hearts, minds and souls. They are not giving Me a moment's chance! When they do listen, they then wish for Me to *speak* to them!

EVERYTHING CENTERS AROUND THEM. Do they not know that I speak to those who want nothing of themselves, because these are the ones who want everything for everyone else?

I am directly saying that I want people to be intimate with Me, but INTIMACY IS INVERSELY RELATED TO SELF-CENTEREDNESS AND SELF IMAGE! The greater their selfishness and pride, the less they are intimate. The greater their love, the less they are self-centered, and the more they are intimate.

It has been very important that I clearly speak today on what I have dictated to you. Bring My people home, child. The comfort of their home awaits them.

SIMPLICITY

DECEMBER 24, 1989

My dear child, so many of My people mistake simpleness with simple mindedness and ignorance! I have said many times: 'I wish for My people to have simplicity!' Allow Me to define the difference, and make clear My terms for My people.

Simplicity is a state of quality of purity and naturalness.

It is NOT simple mindedness. Simple mindedness is a state of foolishness and ignorance. Ignorance is a lack of knowledge. It is a state of being without knowledge. I have asked My people to be simple, not ignorant!

I never said that to be simple, you must be poor, did I? So many of My people believe and associate simpleness with materialistic values. Simplicity and poverty are not one in the same. There are many of My poor beloved ones who lead very complex lives! Simplicity is the lack of complexity.

Any of My people who say, 'you need to lead a simple life,' suggesting monetary values, do not understand what simpleness truly means! The love of money will control you and manipulate you into leading a complex life, but money itself does not identify a lack of simplicity!

My people need to understand these differences. I am not calling My people to simple mindedness, or lack of knowledge. I am calling My people to knowledge and to life without complexity. I am not calling My people to ignorance. I am calling My people to a state of being of purity, especially during this tiding of joy, My birth. I wish for My people to understand, clearly, the significant difference between simplicity, simple mindedness and ignorance.

DAY OF MY BIRTH

DECEMBER 25, 1989

My dear child, what a glorious day; and one on which I come bringing you tidings of joy. This joy is for all My people. I love them, and rejoice in those who have chosen eternal life.

The purpose of My birth, to save My beloved ones and free them from sin and grant them salvation, is fulfilled this day, the day of My birth! Each day is a rebirth for all those who desire life in Me. But this day, 2000 years ago, My Father granted salvation for all through Me! MY BIRTH WAS YOUR SALVATION; MY SUFFERING, YOUR REDEMPTION.

Now the angels sing songs of joy for all who, this day, are

born in Me. I send My peace, and rejoice in all who have chosen eternal life, regardless of their religion. Those who have chosen eternal life, have chosen Me, for only I can provide true eternal life in My Father.

I WISH FOR MY PEOPLE TO KNOW THIS DAY THEY ARE NOT ALONE! REJOICE IN THE GOOD NEWS OF YOUR LIFE. REJOICE, FOR THE NEWBORN BABE IS ALIVE, AND REIGNS FOR ALL ETERNITY. REJOICE, FOR THIS DAY THE FATHER HAS GIVEN ME, YOUR SAVIOUR, TO THE WORLD. COME ALL YE, WHO DESIRE LIFE, AND RECEIVE IT. WITH ME THERE IS NO DEATH, ONLY LIFE; PURITY OF LIFE LIKE A NEWBORN BABE.

It is today I have taken many souls into My Kingdom, especially the forgotten ones! Thank you for your prayers, for these souls have been exalted and glorified on this day, the day of My birth. I am your Jesus Who wishes to give to all. I am not asking anything of anyone, other than to love and be pure. I wish to give to all. Please graciously accept, and live!

Thank you for loving My people. As you love Me, you love them. As you deny yourself for Me, you give to them, and I bless you in thanksgiving. Rejoice, your newborn Babe is born and alive!

CONVERSION—A SLOW PROCESS!

DECEMBER 31, 1989

My dear child, I wish to describe today the path of conversion. As you pray for conversion, the seed is sown in the soil. Conversion is a silent process, only one which I see. Once the seed is sown, the process is slow, slow in order to be nourished and to grow into blossom. As My people convert, they must absorb and accept the seed. Then, silently, they reflect, and slowly grow!

That is why I have said, 'IT IS NOT NECESSARY TO VERBALLY DEBATE ABOUT CONVERSION OR ON WHAT

IS RIGHT OR WRONG ACCORDING TO YOUR STANDARDS!'
Once the seed is sown into the heart, the soil becomes rich
and silently changes the person by perfecting the soul. If the
seed is not sown, then try again and again, until there is
no mistake that the soil is too bad to accept the seed. The
soil is man's heart. The seed, My goodness. Once the seed
is sown, My goodness spreads through the field and kills
the weeds of wickedness.

It is a slow process, for weeds are difficult to eliminate,
for they tend to grow back. But goodness is their poisonous
venom, inviting them to grow fully, so that the root will be
destroyed!

Remember, silence is conversion's patron! If you think your
fellow brethren are not converted, know your thoughts are
deceiving. Once the seed is sown, silently and at My pace,
will the fruit ripen, but all shall be ripe at harvest time! Man
does not know what phase of conversion his fellow brethren
are journeying. **Only I know!** Only the seed knows the stage
of growth. However, pray for all, and this shall fertilize the
soil.

Know, as sinners convert, the more will loving grace and
tender words and loving actions from My people assist in
conversion. This type of loving grace makes the sinners weep
and encourages them in their journey. Never condemn, for
I love all the bad and the good. It is through love the sinner
repents and does so silently! That is the beauty of conversion. It is a journey you must take alone to fully embrace
the intimacy of My eternal Father.

If a sinner laughs in your face and chastises you, simply
remain loving and silent. The laughter will turn to tears of
joy as he weeps in gratitude for planting My seed. Never
argue or return slandering words. Always love and pray that
the seed is fertilized.

That is all for today, My people, I bless them this night
as this decade ends and the Age of My Divine Mercy com-
mences! Peace to all for eternity!

THE VINE

My dear child, so many of My people have perturbations of worries, anxiety and fear. The Word of God is not of perturbations, but of freedom! Those who feel bound by these feelings are allowing the deceit of the evil one to cause turmoil.

I am the Vine which blossoms ripe fruit, not the tree whose roots suffocate the vine! My people are the leaves and the grapes of My Vine. My Father is He Who tills the soil, fertilizing and watering. Those on My Vine, who fall, are suffocated by the root. The root is their lack of faith.

It is like the parable of the man who had a vineyard and was successful in growing ripened grapes until one season the leaves of his vine did not blossom fruit. This man tried pruning his vines and listened to the advice of many in order to restore his vines. However, to no avail. He was unsuccessful, and his vineyard was dying! The man then noticed the tree he had planted next to the vines, which was lovely and strong as ever before! He also noticed the tree continued to gorw, but not the vines. If the soil was bad, should not the tree lose its leaves and the bark begin to dry? So, he exclaimed, it is the roots of this tree which have suffocated my vines, denying my leaves to blossom and my fruit to ripen. I shall dig deep into the soil, and cut the roots and kill this tree so that my vineyard will regain life! And so the man completed what he promised. The tree died and the next season his vineyard grew the sweetest grapes, and his harvest was full. It is the same with My people today. They are My fruit of the vine and their perturbations are the roots of little faith and trust, which suffocate them, denying them the richness to ripen fully and blossom. If they know the root to all evil, they can cut it, releasing them from its grip. Oh, then how the vines will blossom and the harvest bear sweet fruit!

If My people ask My Father, the One Who tills the soil, to cut the roots, the roots will never grow again. He will turn the remaining roots, which were cut, into the fertilizer of the soil!

Absorb what I have said, and reach deep within your heart. There the vine rests and receives the nutrients of life. Peace, My dear one, peace!

THE LOVE OF JESUS

JANUARY 4, 1990

My dear child, My people are not yet convinced of My great love for them, for if they really accepted My love, they would be pure of mind and honest. If they truly recognized My love for them, individually, they would be at peace, happy, and filled with trust. They would want to be like Me!

What does it take to convince My people of My great love? I love the good and the bad, even the bad who do not know Me! BUT I SEE THE LOVE MY PEOPLE HAVE FOR ME BY THE WAY THEY TREAT THEIR BROTHERS. My good continue to be slashed by the dishonesty of the bad.

I am here to warn My people, as a watchman warns the troops before battle! **Take heed, all ye who live deceitfully.** You who are bad and know Me, but do not turn to good, it would be better for you had you never known of My goodness. You who have good in you, but have begun to live deceitfully and dishonestly, it would be better had you not known Me. For those who are good and do deceitful acts will be judged as if they were not righteous. The good deeds accredited to them will not be acknowledged! But those, who are righteous and holy in Me, shall receive their reward without punishment! For what is due to man for his unjust ways, shall be fulfilled as promised by My Father.

Justice will be fulfilled as decreed. Those, who love and

live in faith, have no need to fear, for My seal of protection is on them. Remember, there is no justice in fear. FEAR IS NOT OF ME! If you live in Me and I in you, then you will not fear or allow perturbations of fear to cause you undue duress.

ORDINARINESS

JANUARY 8, 1990

My dear child, today I wish to speak of ordinariness. My people think that, in order to gain the Kingdom of God, they need to be extraordinary and to be recognized by man as a martyr! This is not so! I called all to be saintly in their ordinariness! This is also one of the reasons I have selected you through whom I speak My lessons. If I listen to you and give to you in your ordinariness, would I not listen and give to all My people, if there is not partiality in My love?

Many of My people attempt to conquer the world, and wish to do too many things at a rapid pace! **It is only I Who can conquer the world!** It is necessary to go slowly, and at My pace, if you are to conquer with Me! I am here for all My people and I do not, I repeat, do not favor one over the other! All are blessed in My eyes, who seek the goodness of My Father.

I WISH FOR MY PEOPLE TO KNOW THAT I AM WITH THEM AT ALL TIMES, EVERY MOMENT OF EVERY DAY, NOT ONLY TIMES OF PRAYER! I am with them when they are at home conversing, laughing, arguing, loving, working and crying. Is that not ordinary, daily activity? Is that not a simplicity in functioning very ordinarily with Me in the midst of their presence?

As My people turn to Me, they desire to please Me by doing extraordinary tasks. They wish to go out of their way to please Me in order that they may seek My favor and My peace. **It is I Who wish to give**, and it is in their ordinariness that I provide for them!

Ordinariness is loving, laughing, living pure lives, crying, working and growing. It is not chastising, swearing, blaspheming or drunkenness. I do not wish for My people to stop functioning in their daily activities because they have been found by Me! I wish for all to carry on lovingly, accepting My many gifts. This is the ordinariness of which I am speaking. I wish for all to reflect upon My friendship. Am I their friend? What is a friend? How do you treat a friend? Are not friends ordinary and simple? Are they not patient, loving and devoted? Are they not opinionated, yet lend a listening ear? Will they not allow themselves to be corrected?

I am a God Who loves ordinariness. I listen, am loving and patient. I am devoted and simplistic. I AM REAL! I am comforted, even when My beloved ones take a fall, for their fall develops tears of growth! Is it not ordinary to fall, to grow, to fall and to grow some still?

My point today, My child, is that I love My people in their ordinariness. I am not looking for martyrs. **I am looking for simplicity and dedication to friendship.** I am looking for honesty, openness and growth, all ordinary ways which will be extraordinary in My sight! Do not out-do yourselves in love, My people, but simply MAKE LOVE YOUR WAY OF LIFE. Do not out-do one another by noticeably doing good for others. It is in the quietness of love and simpleness, that good is accomplished. I tell you, it is better to do good for someone quietly, without recognition, than to love with recognition. The glory given to My Father in this form is immeasurable.

Therefore, My dear ones, do not despair. Your walk with Me is one of growth and living your lives in the ordinariness of My love, living simply, honestly, lovingly and purely. This is the ordinariness in My sight that makes you extraordinary in the sight of My Father. Peace, My loved ones, peace.

DEEDS

JANUARY 10, 1990

My dear child, **the deeds of My people reflect their goodness in Me.** Words are of little value unless the action speaks the truth of the word. If your behavior is haughty and your words are loving, is that not a contradiction of My truth? If My people believed in My truth, My word, their actions would reflect their belief. That is how you decipher the true prophets from the false ones! **Deeds speak the truth.** Those who live in Me, live My Word, and their actions affirm the truth of My Word.

Haughtiness and disrespectful behavior to others and to yourself are deeds which confirm falsehood and deceitfulness. The true follower accepts the Word, and allows the Word to develop within them. The Word reflects in His follower's actions. How many today do you witness of promising words, but little trust, and deeds which fail the Word? There are many who desire, initially, to be My follower, but so few who walk the Word because of their underdeveloped respect for themselves and others and, worse still, their lack of devout willingness to allow Me to develop within them mature behavior. Following My Word is going beyond the initial step of desire by speaking promising words. It is affirming the Word through deeds. That is the final truth. Are the deeds respectful or disrespectful? Are they pure or unclean? Are they loving or deceitful? Are they honest or dishonest?

The deed reflects not only the truth of the Word, but reveals the depth of devotion. Are you devoted to My Word at moments of YOUR DESIRE? Do you say you are devoted, but your thoughts and actions speak otherwise by condemning those who appear harmful? Do you love the poorly dressed as the well dressed, or the ignorant as well as those who converse fluently? Do you say you are My follower and live the truth of My Word, but judge and, privately in your inner thoughts, condemn the minority? That is the disgust of your world.

How many live deceiving themselves that they are pure and belong to Me, yet turn around by their deeds and scandalous affairs, living falsely? Let Me tell you something, child. You cannot be called a child of God, and gain the Kingdom, unless your deeds are as pure as My Word! When I say, 'you,' child, I mean all My people, for when I speak to you, I speak to the world. How wretched you are to claim purity as if it were deserving of you when the deed is not pure! When the deeds reflect purity AT ALL TIMES, then you are deserving of purity and the Word.

I AM THE WORD! If you wish to be My follower, you will pray for inner growth development, and accept My truth by living the Word through your actions. I tell you, if you are loving to those with whom you are acquainted and distant to those whom you do not know, or even judge them as an enemy, you cannot be My follower! For those who follow Me are pure love, and their deeds speak the truth of My Word.

That is what I desire to say to My people this day. The choice is yours. Do you truly wish to be My follower? **If so, is your 'yes' one proclaimed through your lips, or is it lived through your deeds?** Your words will never speak the truth. Only your deeds can speak the truth of the Word.

HATRED

JANUARY 14, 1990

My dear child, how I suffered for My people at the time of My delivery to My people to be crucified. How heavy was My cross, brushing splinters into My flesh. Yet, I carried it because of My great love for My people.

I want all to be free, but they have bound their freedom with their law! You are slaves in a concrete world, and your spirits suffer from the lack of freshness and beauty. Oh, how My people are slaves to their world.

I wish to speak today of the hatred of man. Man was created in love; to love with freedom, and to be loved. Their spirits were created to develop and grow in this love and to maintain the wholeness and freshness of youth. Today, even with My lessons and the gift of My Mother which I have given, men (both genders) continue to hate, despise, resent and deplete what little source of love remains. My people continue to fight, kill and attack others. They cripple the old and they batter the young. They want control of their lives, but they cannot control their emotions and temper! They continue to function from impulse, instead of allowing Me to develop goodness within them, and to bring them My peace. My people live with skepticism, and trust little in Me and their brothers. They live in fear and in remorse. What value has resulted in their world from their hatred and lack of interest in loving one another? None, I tell you! There is no value in hatred or in hating! **There is only value in love!** I have told you that resentfulness, the poisonous venom, leads to jealousy and hatred. When there is hatred, only evil exists.

Hatred kills and inspires death. Hatred is darkness and a merciless sword. All, who walk in hatred, walk with the sword of death! THE SWORD KILLS OTHERS AND, IN ITS MOMENT OF PLEASURE, KILLS THE BEARER OF ITS GRIP! There is little hope for those who desire to walk the path of hatred. Terminate hatred by awakening to ill feelings of resentfulness and jealousy. Allow Me to cure and resoil the seed of love! It will restore you to health, and develop into irresistible beauty. Be aware of hatred and its coy elements of disillusion! Be on your guard always, for it will attack without a moment's notice. Pray, and allow Me to protect you and nourish you. Be what true beauty is...LOVE!

ABUSE

JANUARY 16, 1990

My dear beloved one of mercy, how it grieves Me to see how My people show their love and mercy. They neglect their children, beating them, yes beating, child, and denying them growth in love! They verbally and physically batter, not only the young, but the old. Is this mercy? How, child, would you have Me have mercy on them, if they cannot have mercy?

I have been teaching My people throughout the ages the importance of their salvation through love and mercy, and their deeds speak of their thoughts on My teachings!

I give the gift of love, and they take it upon themselves to destroy all dignity of life. What possesses My people to take their anger and aggressions out on the meek, weak and little, grieves My heart. It tears and bleeds for them. These same people, who are to be called children of God, strip all hope of salvation by their evil deeds. They cannot be called 'children of God,' for to be a child of God, you must love as children, not endanger them! You must be childlike, and pure as children.

Never, never have I said that to discipline a child you must beat him!

Never, ever have I praised malicious acts of sexual abuse.

Discipline is achieved with love, and love only.

Correction is accomplished only through love.

Physical love, which joins man and woman together in sacramental marriage, comes from PURE love, and should continue and never be expressed in the form of molestation of the young or sexual abuse of children!

My child, how it grieves Me that these are MY PEOPLE who have allowed such degrading evil to possess them! They have no sense of dignity, and do not even know the value of dignity! These are the people who need to learn what pure love is. THESE ARE MY PEOPLE WHO NEED TO FORGIVE AND LOVE THEMSELVES! These people are not walking on rope, but are walking on string! These are My people I wish to come home to Me, so that I can restore their dignity and goodness.

ABUSE IS SACRILEGIOUS. Verbal, mental, physical abuse of the young, the old and the children is horrifying in the eyes of God. My Father abhors those who do not love, for those who do not walk in love, walk in darkness and death.

Make this known, child. Every person who abuses and batters anyone, elderly or young, shall pay the price marked in the eyes of My Father until every cent worth of abuse is exchanged into the equivalence of love. . .not by the eyes of man, but by the eyes of My Father!

Take heed, My people, for it is by your own will that you walk such treacherous turf! If you wish to be My people, you will head My words. Stop, or there will be no consequences for stopping My Father's actions in defense of the innocent!

Remember, love is sacred, for I am love!

NEGLECT

JANUARY 21, 1990

My child, My people live as if they are the only ones of worth! They are the center, and the ones of value. There are so many of My elderly who are lonely and desolate, because they are not noticed as contributing to society! They lose their dignity because they are treated as having little value or worth. I want all My people to love, and know that all are of value to Me!

My child, if you go into a large room, filled with people you do not know, should that make a difference in how people should perceive or treat you? It should not, but in today's structured and concrete world, it has! The old receive little recognition as being valued unless their worth is of monetary value. People treat each other as aliens, unless they know them! This results in inhumane gestures. People begin to feel useless, unloved and of little worth. Especially My old ones are neglected.

Child, the body may wither and grow old, but the soul remains young, always! I wish for My people to stop seeing the body superficially, and look at others by looking into their hearts! This will prevent all from experiencing unworthiness and neglect. Do not look at age, but at the heart's intent! Treat all with goodness. Treat all as being of value.

People are not inanimate objects or programmed robots. They are people created in My likeness! All are to be loved, appreciated and treated with dignity. This is how you gain the Kingdom...LOVE! It is the key which unlatches the gate!

If you love, you will treat others with dignity, and they will feel loved, wanted and of value to mankind. Reach out to one another with love, and stop being around only the ones with whom you feel comfortable! Communicate with all, and enjoy friendships. Reach out to all, not limiting yourself to those of your desire. Neglect is killing freedom! Do not neglect others, love them!

EUCHARIST / PRESENCE

JANUARY 24, 1990

My dear child, today I wish to speak further on the Eucharist, My Presence in the host you receive.

My dear one, how I long for My people to come and receive Me openly and sincerely. I wish for them to tell Me their most intimate feelings, thoughts and worries. I wish for them to share their joyful events, their sorrows and their struggles. I long to advise them, counsel them and comfort them. Oh, if only they would realize **it is I** they receive and not a piece of man-made host. **It is I, in My true presence, Who dwells in you each time you receive Me.**

So many of My people and My priests simply, routinely, go through the motions. So many of My people, who are My beloved ones, are so entangled and afflicted with self issues! They do not come to share with Me, or allow Me to comfort or counsel with My love. They complain of their own afflictions.

It is time My people know the truth, and listen to Me! I am here for them.

It is I Who humbles Myself to be consecrated to them!

Could they give Me the moment to receive My consecration, and allow My presence to absorb their being?

If My dear people truly recognized Me in the host, they would not be so quick to leave, and wander in their thoughts after receiving My Precious Body and Blood. It is only confirmation on how many of My people go through habitual motions and routine actions, instead of true devotion and dedication! Where is their commitment? I am committed to them. I respect them. Cannot they be loyal to true friendship? I wish to assist them and help them in their times of need. They must allow Me, and listen to Me. How, child, do you listen?

Another question many of My people ask: 'how can I listen? What are the signs? How do I know I am being obedient and listening?'

My response is: 'how can I tell them, if when they come to receive Me, they do not take the time to allow Me to instruct, counsel, guide or fill them with My love? To listen, is to firstly, absorb Me, and to allow Me to fill you with My love. That is the first step. SPEAK TO ME OPENLY, SINCERELY, TRUTHFULLY AND INTIMATELY. STOP BEING OBSESSED WITH SELF-IMAGE, PROBLEMS AND DAILY OCCURRENCES. Come openly to Me, and talk to Me! Then My peace will slowly be absorbed into you, and you will know that your hearts are primed for counsel!

It begins with Eucharist for all those who desire reception of Me, and it continues with respectful mannerisms and devoted faithfulness!

OBEDIENCE

JANUARY 28, 1990

My dear child, I, your Jesus, have humbled Myself to be in your presence now to give another lesson to My people. It is a lesson on obedience, divine obedience.

If My people obeyed Me by trusting in Me, they would be released from their fear, which enslaves them. Divine obedience is the greatest gift My people could give My Father, far greater than sacrifice! Obedience is devotion and love and mercy which My Father graciously accepts and reciprocates in rewarding one hundred fold! Obedience is being open to My words, accepting them and allowing My love to mold you into eternal perfection. Obedience is growth and, with growth, accompanies imperfections and failings! These shortcomings perfect you when you allow Me to strengthen you and teach you. Acceptance in divine obedience to Me allows you to grow and live in the holiness of My Spirit.

A MAJOR FACTOR IN THE GROWTH OF OBEDIENCE IS PATIENCE. In the excitement of growth, it is necessary to grow at My pace! If you allow pride to enter and control you, it will deceive you, and it will destroy the seed of obedience.

Obedience is accepting the characters of My people for who they are, and not imposing upon them to be who you think they should be! Obedience is total acceptance, humility, love, mercy and thankful praise in prayer for correction. Obedience results in peace.

All who are obedient to My Father trust in Me, and are peace filled people, because they live in unity with Me. It is accepting Our plan with trust in a secure future. No matter how large the waves of life, the path of protection and security will take you safely through all treacherous waters!

GROWTH

FEBRUARY 1, 1990

My dear child, **it is I, your Lord, Who comes to you.** Even in your illness do I live in you and give you the strength to take down My words for My people.

You have noticed that three things happen when people find out that I come to you. They are either afraid; do not care; or are overwhelmed and cling to you, as if you were a link to Me.

I tell you, it was the same with Me! Either My people were afraid that I was possessed by demons; they did not care; or they panicked to be in My presence, fearing that I would not heal them! Do you know the ones who tore My heart the most? It was the same group of people that makes your heart bleed, the ones who do not care!

Remember My saying, 'there is no middle of the rope, only two ends?' How I long for My people. My heart bleeds for them, and desires to give to them, but those, who do not care, do not even wish to receive. They do not care at all. Especially My gifts would only be a burden to them! That is why your heart suffers, because My heart suffers!

I would like to tell My people that I am here to divide the good from the bad! Take the time to sort in your heart My words, and make your decision. If you have questions, ask! If you come to Me in private prayer, I will show you.

Tell My people My words. MY PEOPLE NEED TO GROW IN ME, and I will give them strength and knowledge. But with growth comes imperfections and failures, which I allow to strengthen and mold My people into My perfection of holiness. Those who suffer and allow Me to suffer with them, are strengthened and grow. Their suffering only sanctifies them. Those who choose to suffer without Me, suffer great turmoil at their own wish, because they will not allow Me to carry their cross. Their path of growth is long, tedious, and strenuous. Pray for them!

Growth is essential in My journey. This spiritual maturity is one through which I can take you. Men cannot judge the spirituality of their brethren. Focus on your own spirituality with Me, and do not look at another's journey. Be careful and on guard against judging others, especially in their spirituality. Only the Trinity knows the degree of strength of the soul.

My words today are a lesson to My people on growth, which is so essential in My journey of holiness. Do not despair over your imperfections or failures. Do not struggle with your perturbations. Know I am with you, if you allow Me to assist you in your growth to divine holiness.

Remember My words, 'if you try and fail, you have not failed in My eyes, but have won favor in the sight of My Father!' Be strong, and take one moment at a time. Live in the moment, day by day!

FOLLOW THE WORD

FEBRUARY 6, 1990

My dear child, today there is a great deal I wish to make known to My people. I do not keep the truth from My people. I am a dignified God Who gives and listens! My words are made known, not as secrets, but as justification for worthiness.

Throughout the ages I selectively chose My words to My people, for their unworthiness did not justify them to hear or know the Word. Then the blood from the Word became their redemption! Today, unworthiness prevents total knowledge of My Word, but I have granted to all who desire to know the Word, to come with open hearts and minds.

I am not a secretive God! Secrets are secrets, but My words are for all who desire them in order to cleanse themselves. All who acknowledge Me will follow My ways, My word. All who follow the Word, are justified in worthiness in the sight of the Father. All who are worthy of Me, will carry their cross (whether it be illness, heroism, finances, renunciation, mourning, spiritual depression or sadness) with resignation and acceptance, for it is by the will of God that their cross is given!

Today, there are many who would like to know the Word of God, but only a minimal amount will actually acknowledge the Word by following and practising His Way! The Word is not secret. All who know the Word, know His secrets; however, there are few who know Him!

I have told you that all who accept you, My prophet, My disciple, accept Me, for I live in you and We are one in the Father. Those who accept a prophet are prophets themselves, for THE LIKE KNOW EACH OTHER AND ARE ONE IN THE SPIRIT OF MY FATHER. Those who accept My chosen disciples are also disciples, for they are of the same Shepherd! If you acknowledge a just man, you also are a just man. If you acknowledge and accept the evil one, you are of dark spirit! **What you choose to acknowledge by faith is what you are!** If you wish to come with Me, know My word and acknowledge Me by following My word. If you wish to go the evil way, then I shall allow you to bite into darkness and know the deceit of the evil one's words!

I am telling My people, child, that all who desire goodness need only come to Me. Once they come to Me by asking Me to live in them, no danger of eternal darkness can possess them. All who desire darkness will be granted it. But all who remain with Me cannot be possessed and need not be afraid. All who do not desire Me nor invite My protection are prey!

Come to Me, My people! Trust in Me, and do not fear. MAN IS MAN'S ENEMY! Put your trust in the Word, not in man! If you trust in the Word and the man who lives in the Word, you will both share in comfort and peace by jointly trusting in the Word! This allows you to trust in your brethren.

You say, 'profound,' child. I say, 'simply the truth!' Put all your trust in Me. Show Me your trust by fully living in your faith. Do not allow even your closest relative to steer you away from Me! IF YOU CHOOSE YOUR MOTHER, YOUR FATHER, SIBLINGS OR CHILDREN OVER ME, THEN YOU HAVE NOT CHOSEN ME!

I must be all of you, or I can be none of you. If I am all of who you are, then those you love are embraced by divine serenity, protection, peace and dignity. Remember, I have come into the world to divide the good from the bad.

ALL WHO DESIRE ME, COME FORWARD! Say, 'yes' to Me, and invite Me into your heart before it is too late, and you have been bitten by the evil one! Divine protection rests in Me. Won't you, please, come and rest in My heart of peace? Come to eternity. Come to eternal peace. Come into My Heart!

Ad Deum, child. (Ad Deum is explained by Jesus to me as, 'Back to God I return!')

WILL OF GOD

FEBRUARY 10, 1990

My child, if My people will open their hearts to the Will of My Father, they will receive the peace which their souls desire. The Will of My Father is the most critical ingredient to your happiness!

If only My people would accept His Will for them, how endless their happiness would be! Do you know the Will of God, and accept it?

If you know the Word, you know the Will, for I am the Word and all who know Me know Who sent Me and His Will! Trusting in Me is knowing Me. Living My way is knowing Me. Accepting with joy all that is sent you, is accepting the Will of My Father. If you live in Me, you will live in My peace. If you live in My peace, all suffering is joy, for it is redemptive. My peace brings discernment and divine protection. Accepting My Will for you is trusting in Me.

If I have told My people of My great love, then trusting in Me would indicate their trust in My care for them. If they trusted in My care, they would accept the Will of My Father, planned for them. They do not live in peace because they will not accept the Will of God, since they do not trust in Me! The Will goes back to trust. All surrounds the trust My people have for Me. They are afraid I will not care for them. They are afraid I will forget them. They are afraid that My Will for them will conflict with their will! If they are afraid of My Will conflicting with theirs, they do not trust Me because My Will only leads to peace and happiness.

How My people struggle because they do not trust. It is the Will of God which will free them! If you know Me, you will trust Me and will accept with peace what is deigned for you. You will know it is the Will for you because, if you know Me, then you know I live in you and would not allow harm to come to you. The evil one can irritate you and attempt to confuse you from knowing the Will, but, if you ACCEPT WITH PEACE, then only goodness will result and His Will be done!

PEACE IS THE KEY TO KNOWING THE WILL. If you live in Me, you live in peace and will accept with peace. Evil cannot live in peace because evil does not know peace! If evil cannot live in peace, you know you are doing the Will of My Father.

My child, this lesson on the Will of My Father is so necessary. IT ALL COMES DOWN TO TRUST: TRUSTING IN ME; LIVING IN ME; LIVING IN MY PEACE; ACCEPTING WITH PEACE THE WILL.

The outcome of God's Will will ALWAYS BE PEACEFUL, and result in your happiness. It also gives you glory because, by doing the Will of God, you give Him glory! If you give My Father glory, you have given Me glory. If you live in Me, you have, in turn, received glory yourself!

I HAVE CHOSEN YOU

FEBRUARY 12, 1990

My dear child, as My people accept My lessons and grow in Me, there is something very important they must realize. It is My joy to come to My people and teach them; however, they need to know that **it is I Who have chosen them!** As they grow in My words and are filled with My love, they begin to think that they have the answers for others in their journey of life. They begin to plan and announce to others, whether they be friend or enemy, what is right or wrong. They even begin to speak as if they know of what is to come. My love awakens and fills them with knowledge, but they need to keep My knowledge in perspective or it will deceive them!

My people plan events for other people's lives. They think they know with certainty when one of Mine is to die! Beware! Grow in My love. Allow Me to guide you. Allow Me to be your God. Allow Me to plan your life's events.

If you truly grow and follow My ways, you will follow the example of My Mother. Contemplate how she loves Me by serving Me quietly and obediently. She never spoke to anyone in a manner which was authoritative. She never said what would happen to anyone or told anyone they were not living correctly. She always showed her love by listening, assisting, and praying for them. If you are truly growing in My love, know that I found you. You did not find Me! Live as My mother lived for Me.

My people are still filled with so much judgment. I tell you, child, no one knows what event will happen, worldly or even simply in someone's life! Only I know and dictate according to My Father's glory.

Accept with peace and joy My presence in your hearts and learn to love openly without judgment or condition for your spouse, family, friends, co-workers and enemies. Maintain equanimity in all matters and ALLOW ME TO BE YOUR GOD. If you accept only what you wish, and deceive yourselves by knowing the time and events in other people's lives, then you are playing God!

If you want to receive My glory and grow in My light, accept these words: SPEAK LESS AND LOVE MORE BY LISTENING AND PRAYING. OPEN YOUR HEARTS TO AB-SORB MY LOVE FOR YOU AT THIS VERY MOMENT. DO NOT PLAY LEADER, FOR THIS WILL ONLY CAUSE DECEP-TION AND CONFUSION. LET THINGS BE AND ACCEPT. SIM-PLY ACCEPT WITH JOY, MY LOVE FOR YOU. REMEMBER, MY PEOPLE CANNOT HELP ME, THEY CAN SERVE ME BY ALLOWING ME TO LOVE THEM. DO NOT TAKE MATTERS INTO YOUR OWN HANDS BECAUSE YOU ARE CERTAIN OF WHAT IS TO COME OR WHAT SHOULD COME. PLEASE, PLEASE, PLEASE, MY PEOPLE, ALLOW ME TO BE YOUR GOD. YOU ARE NOT MINE! I LOVE YOU AND SPEAK THIS WAY IN ORDER FOR YOU TO REFLECT ON YOUR GROWTH AND LOVE FOR ME. WHERE ARE YOU IN YOUR JOUR-NEY? ARE YOU OPEN? ARE YOU VERBOSE? ARE YOU CER-TAIN THAT YOU KNOW WHAT IS THE NEXT EVENT TO HAPPEN IN YOUR BROTHERS' LIVES? REFLECT! ARE YOU ALLOWING ME TO GUIDE YOU AS I HAVE PLANNED, OR ARE YOU DECEIVING YOURSELVES BY GUIDING YOUR-SELVES? ARE YOU ALLOWING ME TO BE YOUR GOD? ARE YOU? OR ARE YOU NOT?

Look into your heart and look at the words and actions of your day, and reflect how My mother would respond if she lived and spoke the words you did. There is much I teach

you and, before we go further in your lessons, please, contemplate on the words I have spoken.

I love you, My people. My peace is for you! My words
are for you, and My Kingdom is for you!

USE YOUR FAITH

FEBRUARY 18, 1990

My dear child, why do My people struggle so in their faith?
I have promised them gifts of peace and strength and protection, yet they struggle. They do not persevere. The smallest
trauma weakens their security and trust. That is because of
their weak faith.

My faith is your power! Use the gift of your faith. YOUR
STRUGGLES DO NOT COME FROM ME. YOUR STRUGGLES
ARE YOUR PASSIONS AND DESIRES.

FAITH JUSTIFIES YOU IN ME. It makes you righteous in
the eyes of My Father. My people are so concerned over what
is 'of God' and what is not, that they have deceived themselves. Live in your faith in Me, and be at peace. Trust in
Me and all shall be tended for. Stop judging what others are
doing to you in creating conflicts. Focus on Me and on what
I have planned for you. This is for all My people. How they
wish to control! How confident they are in dictating what is
of God and what is not! My, what authority they have taken
into their own hands! Oh, how they are creating their own
struggles by their passions.

Do not live a life of death! Live in the life of light. Do
not deceive yourselves. Trust in yourselves by trusting in Me.
If you trusted in Me, you would walk in faith and would not
allow your feelings and struggles to deceive you. How many
times have I said that I am with you always, and will protect
and care for you? My love does not and will not change!
I am a loving God, a God Who will not cause harm. If you
love Me and trust Me, you will walk in your faith with Me
and stop causing yourselves inner harm.

Your struggles are those you create and allow! This causes you internal suffering and harm. This does not reflect your faith or trust in Me. Therefore, My people, STOP CAUSING YOURSELVES AND OTHERS SUFFERING BY TELLING OTHERS WHAT IS AND WHAT IS NOT OF GOD! Allow Me to live in you by caring for you. Have faith in Me, and walk in My footsteps. All shall be cared for.

Thank you, My dear ones. I, your Lord, love you and speak words of truth, words to teach you and guide you to eternal life!

UNITY

FEBRUARY 21, 1990

My dear child, how I long for the minds, hearts and souls of My people. If you love your Lord with all of your mind, heart and soul, you cannot be wounded internally. Divine protection seals in My goodness.

The evil one cannot irritate you with confusing thoughts if you have given Me your mind. Those who walk with Me and follow Me harbor pure thoughts. Their temptations can only be short-lived, for evil thoughts are not able to manipulate their actions.

When you give to Me your mind, it is united to Mine. When you give to Me your heart, it is united to Mine. When you give to Me your soul, My Divinity becomes yours! It is so necessary for all three elements to be united in love to Me and the Trinity.

If I have your heart, but not your mind, your struggles will persecute you with the complexity of analysis and acceptance of the truth! You will doubt, and easily fall apart at the simplest comment of mockery. Your heart will suffer tremendously when it is not in unity with your mind. Your deeds reflect the desires of your heart, but also your mind. If your mind harbors impure thoughts and struggles with introspection, then your heart will suffer because this results in conflict.

Give to Me your mind and you will have Mine! Be open

to receive My wisdon. MY WISDOM TEACHES YOU THAT THE HEART, SOUL AND MIND MUST BE ONE IN UNITY TO BE ONE WITH ME. Do not allow your mind to dictate your thoughts with confusion. Be open to Me, and allow My Spirit to replace your thoughts with pure ones. You will have the clarity to resolve solutions to problems.

Unite, My dear, dear people, your minds to your hearts and to your souls!

HONESTY

FEBRUARY 25, 1990

My dear child, I wish to tell My people to be honest with themselves and with others! So many deceive due to the lack of their honesty. Always be truthful.

THE THREE ELEMENTS OF FREEDOM ARE LOVE, PRAYER AND HONESTY! Do not hide from yourself! Be open and honest, and I can mend your hearts and refresh you. You only deceive yourself when you try to mask the truth. I see the hearts of My people. I read them! I know what will happen before they even have knowledge of their personal situations. I created them. I know their souls! By being honest and truthful to yourself, you accept the Will of God and cannot deceive others. Nor can you deceive yourself when you are honest!

There is so much I wish to teach My people. There is so much I wish to give to them. Can they accept Me for Who I Am? Will they accept Me?

To accept Me, you need to be honest and truthful. How can I dwell in you if there is deceit? I AM TRUTH. I AM HONESTY. I AM LOVE.

If you are honest with yourself, you will experience freedom. I read your hearts. If you are masking the truth from yourself, you cannot accept Me, the God of truth. Only when you are honest with yourself, can you be honest with others. If you cannot be honest with others because you are afraid of them, then you do not trust Me nor are you allowing Me to dwell in you. ONLY THE TRUTH CAN FREE YOU!

It is a decision mankind must make. Will they decide for Me or for deceit? There is no need to exaggerate your stories in order to persuade someone or to make the outcome one to be in your favor. This only prevents growth and peace! Your own dishonesty will only turn on you and pierce your heart with a two edged sword.

Be careful, My beloved ones, you are walking on ice! Your deceit will only cause you to fall through and freeze your soul! Stop deceiving yourselves by attempting to convince others with words of dishonesty. Stop seeking the acceptance of man, but seek acceptance from God. Humble yourselves before the sight of Him Who sent Me! Seek first His Kingdom in truth.

I live in entirety in those who desire and accept Me. TO ACCEPT ME, YOU MUST LIVE IN TRUTH, FOR I AM TRUTH.

This is your lesson today, child, for My people. Always seek and be truth. If you do this, you will always live in Me, and I in you in the oneness of the Trinity. Bless you, My child, and I bless the world through you as you bring them to Me daily! Peace! Ad Deum.

LOOK AT THE MESSAGE

MARCH 4, 1990

My dear child, the sorrow in My heart was one of the most painful symptoms of My Passion. How I tried to teach My people, with the little time I had, of the goodness of My Father and the many facets to freedom. I suffered frustration because so many people could not understand My message. Many did not want to be saved and many were looking at the surface of My words. The pain and frustration of My heart was great. It is like that now. My people look at My words, not at My message.

Here I am, dictating words of truth and the keys to the Kingdom, and so many skeptics and scholars look at My words for errors instead of reading them with their heart, seeking the message!

The pain in My heart still exists. Do not My people realize how much I love them to ask My Father's permission to be able to speak to them in the form of these lessons, so that they can learn and be with Me in the glory of everlasting life?

Tell My people to look at My message and not to be frightened that these words may not be from Me. Begin to apply the principles of My lessons so that I may continue to give more.

IF MY PEOPLE DO NOT WISH FOR ME TO TEACH THEM, THEN I WILL STOP!

I will not infringe upon the free will of My people. I will only continue, if they desire. After this fourth set of lessons, I shall stop giving them for a period of time, to see the effects of My lessons on My people. If I see the desire and change of their hearts, I shall continue. If I do not, the words of My divine holiness shall cease! IT IS MY LAST EFFORT IN GIVING THE OPPORTUNITY TO GRASP SALVATION. If only they knew the depth of My love for them. They would desire to seek Me with all of their strength, if they believed.

So many do not even wish to get involved by reading My messages because they are afraid that it is not I, and are afraid of their credibility from mankind! I still will continue always to love each and every one of My people until the end of time.

This is the lesson: look at My message in My lessons, not at each word! The reason I spoke in many parables was because My people could seek the message of My Father. Now, I speak clearly and simply in order that all may understand My message, and they are looking only at the surface of My words!

Peace to you this day, My dear one, and to all My people.

EXPRESSIONS OF LOVE

MARCH 7, 1990

My dear child, people carry My joy by their facial expressions. Those who walk with Me show their love by their total ambiance. I WISH FOR ALL TO SHOW THEIR LOVE FOR ONE ANOTHER BY SHOWING THEIR LOVE IN THEIR EXPRESSIONS.

If you are at peace, peace will show through your actions and on your face. If you are filled with My joy, My joy will show through your actions and radiate on your face. Those who walk with Me show My divine presence! I wish for all to love. Love is the greatest gift there is! My people need to focus on the grace of love. THERE IS AVERSION, DETACHMENT, AND NEGLECT IN BEING DISINTERESTED! Love is loving the spirit; loving far beyond the body, but loving the spirit, for the spirit is God!

If you love someone, you take interest in that person and have feelings of attachment. If you dislike someone, you have no interest in that person. Is this the love I have taught? Love one another by loving their spirit.

It is like a rose. All the petals are the beauty which surrounds the core of the rose. The core is the Father, and all the petals are the beauty of the Father, His people! The rose flourished in the soft beauty of velvet, with love. When there is no love, the rose dries, and the petals fall, one by one! God is the center of love!

Then there are the father and mother who are procreators of life. Loving them is loving the Father. There are your siblings and blood relatives. Through your blood, you love. I say to love beyond the fact of being related through blood! Love the Spirit and love the Father Who loves in the Spirit.

Taking it to a larger scale: love your neighbors; love your countrymen. These are your neighbors, for you are all one in spirit. Your parents and brothers are neighbors, for their spirit is that of My Father.

When I say love your neighbors, I say to love all, for the Father lives in all and His Spirit is love! I wish for all people to know this love, and to live it.

I give you peace this day, as I always give you My peace. Remember, My love for you, My people, shall never cease!

DISCIPLESHIP

MARCH 12, 1990

My dear one, if My people wish to be My disciples, they must be free in spirit. They must deny the sensual passion of love they have for their spouse, children, brothers and sisters, mother and father. The love they have for their close ones must yield to one love, Mine! They must deny themselves and even 'hate in a holy manner' their being, and surrender to My love. My love is a freedom.

Love your families and close ones by loving their spirit, not with the sensuality of love bound by control. Learn to hate this type of heaviness of love. When I say, 'hate in a holy manner,' I do not mean hatred, I mean denying the passions of love, but loving with the freedom of the Spirit. All must deny himself, and those he loves, in order to follow Me and yield to My love. However, love those by My Spirit.

My disciples must be free like a butterfly. The cocoon and webs, which restrict freedom, are the evil one's tactics of restricting love. Be free by loving My ways and My words, instead of loving the world and people through sensual passion, which controls and paralyzes the spirit. My true followers understand this love and denial. It is their relatives who cause misery of the flesh by wishing to restrict the freedom of their love of the spirit, by controlling and attempting to cause guilt or instill fear!

All must yield to the Father's love, a love that is not of human standards, but one which is of Divine. Those, who know Me, know of My love and accept with humble resignation. It is the only way to freedom.

Man worries far too much! If he worries, he should worry about the richness of virtue. However, mind you, this worry must not be anxious or painful. Good is the enemy of anxiety, fear and haste. To be free, you must be peaceful, peaceful in victory and peaceful in defeat! You must be peaceful at work and be constant and confident. You must be peaceful, even in your tears, when you have displeased God. YOU MUST NOT BE ANGRY WITH YOURSELF WHEN YOU FALL, FOR

ANGER IS ONLY A SYMPTOM OF PRIDE AND LACK OF CONFIDENCE.

When you sin, say, 'Father, forgive me, for I am weak. You are aware of my weakness, which overwhelms me. Help me to be free from the stain of sin, and keep me faithful to your Divine Word.'

My disciples submit freely to this type of love and peacefulness. They walk with Me by the freedom of spirit. They do not deceive themselves by using their handicaps to justify themselves in their feelings of sorrow. If you wish to be My disciple, you will take My words into your heart, and show Me your heart's desire through your actions.

This, child, concludes this lesson today. Receive My blessings on this day of your creation into the world, your birth, and rejoice as you celebrate with My angels in holy song. Peace and Ad Deum.

TRUTH AND HONESTY

MARCH 24, 1990

My dear child, I, your Lord, tell you that many of My people unveil the truth, but many do not accept the truth. They act as if they have no knowledge of the truth. Better not to have any knowledge of the truth than to find it and not acknowledge it! The truth is your sword. Honesty is the weapon which will defend you in battle. Always be on guard!

I liken My people to the fort of God! Keep the fort guarded. Never let your shield down, or the enemy shall come in and strip you of your weapons. When you find you are deprived of your weapon, your heart will surrender and fall into the enemy's hand. Those who walk with Me, are protected from harm! No harm can befall them. UNION WITH GOD IS CERTAINTY OF VICTORY AND ETERNAL ABUNDANCE OF VIRTUES, WHICH LEAD TO AN ETERNAL SEAT IN THE KINGDOM OF GOD!

Always be strong and live in your faith. It is your power. You, My young ones, protect your family with prayer. YOU

ARE THE NEW TOMORROW! Do not allow the evil one to deprive you of your weapons. He wishes for you to think you are weak, so that He can sneak into your house and betray your heart by slaying it with your own weapon! Join in family love and unity. Be holy!

I grant the grace of wisdom and the material necessary for your knowledge, but you must desire holiness, and achieve it through your own merit! Be loyal to the law and practice it in obedience. This is the road of holiness.

My mother was Immaculate because My Father created her soul as such, but it was her loyalty to the law and practice in obedience, which deemed her holy! Seek her as your example to follow in holiness. Be strong, and the treasures you seek shall abundantly be betrothed unto you.

Peace to you this day. Remember, those, who share in My suffering and endure it faithfully, must also share in My joy and My glory. Ad Deum.

THE PASSION OF JESUS

MARCH 30, 1990 and APRIL 18, 1990

My dear child, this lesson for My people is the last lesson of this set. Please write these next words down of My sorrowful passion. My passion consisted of many things, but there are six elements which I wish to make known.

The first was that of My mental anguish. My mental anguish consisted of the conflict between being human—having emotions and the non-emotions of being Divine! The constant knot in My stomach came from being of the Father, yet sharing man's life, having been sent in human form. How many times I knew of My people's dislike, hatred and doubt by experiencing the feelings and sentiments they had for Me. That was My conflict.

The second was the sorrow of My heart knowing the goodness and glory of My Father, but that few desired to know His goodness or seek His glory. The frustration was mixed with sorrow, because of the short time I was granted in which to teach. Yet no one understood Me. My heart was pierced because of My love for My Father and My people, yet their love was conditional! They came to Me in curiosity, in need of physical healing, and whatever personal desire they were seeking at the moment. They could not grasp My words of truth and apply them in search of eternal happiness. That was My sorrow.

The third was My loneliness. The greatest pain and grief was My loneliness, loneliness for My Father, and for My people to know Him. MY LONELINESS CONSISTED OF NOT EVEN FEELING THE PRESENCE OF MY FATHER! The last sorrow was being one of all mankind, yet Divine, without Him Who sent Me. It was unbearable, and faith was the only virtue which showered Me with comfort.

The fourth was temptation. The temptation was threefold. First there was the temptation of exposure, exposing Me as the Messiah, and exposing the glory accompanied with being Saviour. Silent redemption was My mission, to suffer and save all men without exposing the glory of the truth UNTIL THE FINAL MOMENT! Second was the temptation of not contemplating the mission. In My weariness, so many did not understand. Would they ever understand the truth of My Father, and the eternal life available to them? Third was the lifeless sorrow of being no value to My people. My words were merely words to them. Would they ever absorb them, and rejoice in My Father? Was My suffering going to be in vain? NO! But the temptations tormented My heart because that is what man believed and what the evil one desired.

The fifth element was that of fear, fear of conviction. The Son of Man was to be convicted! In the garden, how I prayed that if the moment could pass by, allowing but what the Father's will would be, I would accept! My Father came to Me and, in Our oneness, shared His love for His people, which was My love! The love, being so great, could only result in the salvation of His people through the sacrifice of His Son. The love conflicted with the fear, surpassed it, and comforted Me into a state of being of surrender. The moment was at hand when the Son of Man would sacrifice Himself for mankind, whether mankind was ready for salvation or not! IT WAS MY TOTAL SURRENDERING TO THIS STATE OF BEING WHICH LED TO THE FINAL ELEMENT OF MY PASSION, MY ABANDONMENT.

My abandonment consisted of an empty void of nothingness, lifelessness, emotionlessness and emptiness. My weariness increased to the point of exhaustion. Did My Father abandon Me in My last moments of breath? I was all alone, yet no one to understand My sacrifice and to accept salvation. It was not My wounds which led to My death. It was sheer exhaustion which asphyxiated Me by suffocation. I was too weak to hold My head up any longer. It was with those words, 'Into Your hands I commit My Spirit,' that man would then realize what he had done. The Son of Man would die, only to raise up His Kingdom in three days.

Child, it is with this end of My fourth set of lessons that I wish to tell My people that LIFE EXISTS FOR ALL WHO BELIEVE IN THE TRUTH OF HIM WHO HAS SENT ME.

SLOW DOWN, MY PEOPLE. ENJOY AND APPRECIATE WITH GRATITUDE ALL THE GIFTS AND BLESSINGS MY FATHER HAS GRANTED AND BETROTHED UNTO YOU. TAKE HEED OF HIS WORDS. TAKE THE TIME TO ABSORB THEM AND LIVE THEM. BELIEVE WITH ALL OF YOUR HEART IN YOUR SALVATION, AND BE IMMERSED IN HIS LOVE!

I love you, My dear people; a love which does not suffocate, but gives life.

Come to Me.

Allow Me to come to you.

Open your hearts in willingness, and accept My peace. It is for you.

All I have is for you, My dear ones.

Know I shall never leave you.

I am with you, each one of you who desires Me and will have Me.

All are special in the eyes of God. I am here to purify you and give you all of Me; to protect, guide, comfort and be your strength. Remember the gifts you have are because My Father has granted them to you, and that your power is that which He has allowed you!

Rejoice in Him and be glad.
Sing praises on high to His glorious Name.
I, His Son, am One with Him.
Unite with Us, and be one in the Holy Trinity.
It is today My Mercy sheds in completion of My lessons.
Receive abundantly, and do not fear.
KNOW I AM WITH YOU UNTIL THE END OF TIME.
Peace, My dear, beloved people. Peace to you for all eternity!

VOLUME II

Part II

Messages
From Our Lord and Our Lady

Received by
St. Maria Goretti Parish
Prayer Group

Note:

Since all the words in these messages are
those of Our Lord, or Our Lady, quotation
marks are thus eliminated.

Messages From Our Lord And Our Lady Given Through St. Maria Goretti Parish Prayer Group

JUNE 15, 1989
(MARY)

My children, I am here. Thank you for inviting me.

My dear ones, I wish for you to continue to remain open-hearted. I have spoken of this often because it is so important. Remember you have the choice every day to open your hearts. Please do so daily. Do not come with open hearts on Thursdays only! Remain open-hearted when you leave for your homes and make the commitment daily to be open-hearted to my Son. He will fill you with His love.

My married ones, do not argue with your spouse! Especially over your beliefs. Love, do not argue. It is your love and your actions which shall draw my dear ones to my Son...not your words!

Love, pray and please, I urge you, remain open-hearted so that you will be prepared! Thank you for your response to my call.

JUNE 22, 1989
(MARY)

My dear children, I once again am here with you. Whenever you open your hearts to my Son, you can be sure that I am in your presence, because you allow me.

This week, my children, I ask of you to begin fasting for my Jesus. There are many ways to fast. Go slowly and do not attempt to fast on bread and water if you have not fasted before! You are to be happy when you fast, not gloomy and

73

do not let your peers know you are fasting! Simply do so joyfully. If you begin to fast and pray, I shall help you so your fasting becomes natural. Do not fast more than two times a week! If you cannot fast on bread and water, then delete something of your pleasure and offer it to my Son.

Bless you, my children, and do not fear! Offer everything up to my Son tonight and He shall purify and comfort you. Thank you once again, for your response to my call.

JULY 6, 1989
(MARY)

My dear children, I, your mother, tell you there is no time to waste in your conversion. Please, open your hearts to my Son and pray with all your might to Him for the salvation of this world. Do not be fearful. There is no time for fear! Be strong soldiers, faithful ones, and begin living in His purity. **I cannot stress enough to you the importance of these words!**

Please begin acting as pure soldiers, my angels of love. Put aside your personal desires and seek the desire of my Son. I am here for a purpose. That purpose is to bring you to Him, and to save you...only this!

Thank you, my dear ones, for responding to my call. Our peace is with you.

JULY 13, 1989
(MARY)

My dear children, one year ago I asked several children if they would deny themselves for my Son's glory and suffer much ridicule. They responded joyfully to His service. For one year now I have been preparing them and molding them to be the leaders of my army of which you are all a part.

You must know that these children are not more special than you, but that I and my Son selected them to carry out Our commands because of their youth, strength and energy! Know you are all chosen and are my children, my Son's people. These children have been given symbols which you are to live by, and have been given many special graces of discernment, spiritual healings, emotional healings and physical healings.

In addition, one of these children has been selected by my

Son as a source through which His Divine radiance and mercy shall flow out onto many. These children shall soon be made known to you for they are at the end of their preparation.

My dear children, know We are not asking you to change your way of life, but to change your heart, so that your lives can be lived in happiness. My Jesus wishes for you to be His chosen ones. All who desire Him are chosen!

Thank you, my dear ones, and please, support my children with your love! I tell you that they are working on your behalf for your salvation! My peace be with you.

JULY 20, 1989
(MARY)

My dear children, first always seek the Kingdom of God. Live your lives in the holiness of my Son and seek His Kingdom. I tell you, if you do not seek the Kingdom of God, your prayers are in vain!

He is the truth and all your works should be done to His pleasure. Seek the Kingdom of God first, above all. Thank you, my dear ones, for responding to my call.

JULY 27, 1989
(OUR LORD)

My dear children, today, I again give you My mother. She is My love and My breath! I give you her because you are her loved ones, and her breath of desire. Allow her to be your love and your breath!

She is so beautiful, and is all that I am! Give her honor. When you give her honor, you are giving Me and My Father honor. Our honor will result in your glory!

Thank you for your faith in Our truth. Peace, and My blessings to you.

AUGUST 3, 1989
(MARY)

My dear children, receive my Son through His Eucharist. Receive Him and invite Him to purify, dwell and rest in you.

My children, you do not realize the power of my Jesus in His Eucharist. It is He...in physical form, my Son, your

Jesus, the manna of life! Please, receive Him and allow Him to make you holy!

Thank you, my children, for responding to my call.

AUGUST 10, 1989
(MARY)

My dear children, this week I invite you to ask my Spouse, the Holy Spirit, to dwell in you and guide you. All you need to do is ask Him to dwell in you at the beginning of each morning. He shall watch over you, and you shall see His wondrous works as He guides you this week in your daily lives. There is something for all of you!

PLEASE, do not forget to invite Him daily! PLEASE, invite the Holy Spirit to dwell in you.

Thank you, my dear ones, for your response to my call.

MESSAGE FROM OUR LORD ON THE FEAST OF THE ASSUMPTION

AUGUST 15, 1989
(OUR LORD)

My dear people:

On this, My mother's feast, I wish to share with you My joy, as I celebrate in her goodness, as the Mother of Humankind. Lift your voices and give praise and honor to My mother, for she is your mother, as I have given her to you.

My people, celebrate and open your hearts to her love. Her love grants you your salvation! Be at peace, and know I have gathered your prayers to My most compassionate heart, and shall answer them according to your intimate happiness.

Bless you, My people. My peace I give you.

AUGUST 24, 1989 *(None given for this date)*

AUGUST 31, 1989
(MARY)

My dear children, once again I ask you to take prayer seriously. In these days Satan is trying to cause much harm and disrupt your peace. Please pray with all your heart and take prayer seriously. Do not speak of my messages only. Please, begin to absorb them and live them! Remember, it is not what you say but what you do!

Prayer will bring you to my Jesus and is your protection from Satan. Please pray continuously and know I cannot give you any new messages until you begin to live the current ones!

I love you, my dear ones, and I am praying for you. Thank you for your response to my call.

SEPTEMBER 7, 1989
(MARY)

My dear children, today is the day on which I ask you to fight Satan by loving and accepting one another. Satan cannot and will not win! Love slays him.

Be strong and accept one another. Much glory will be given to you who persevere. Please trust in God. Please seek God and put aside your sentiments and emotions. Please do not argue with one another. All are beautiful in God's eyes.

Seek His Kingdom and fight Satan through loving and accepting one another! Thank you for your response to my call.

SEPTEMBER 14, 1989
(MARY)

My dear children, It is through the blood of my Son that you, His beloved people, have been redeemed. When you *completely* trust in Him, He is able to cure you, heal you and sanctify you in His Spirit.

Please, my dear, dear children, totally trust in my Son. Allow my tears for your sorrow to cleanse you and purify you. I, your Mother of Sorrows, have lived your sorrow, and am here to comfort you. This is my wish for you: total happiness and peace in my Son! Thank you, my dear ones, for your response to my call of total trust.

SEPTEMBER 21, 1989
(OUR LORD)

My dear people, in this, 'My Age of My Divine Mercy,' it is your self-centeredness and soul I have mercy on! It is during this time that I give to you My peace for your devotion to My Father.

The lack of love will continue until My people turn to their God with hope and thanksgiving! I wish for all to be filled with My Spirit of goodness, truth, joy, peace and compassion! I wish for all to receive My love and My mercy. Turn away from your self-righteousness and be righteous in Me, your loving God!

AMEN TO THOSE WHO HEAR MY WORDS AND REJOICE, FOR THEY SHALL INHERIT THE LAND OF THE LIVING!

SEPTEMBER 28, 1989
(MARY)

My dear children, during this age of my Son's Divine Mercy, He sheds upon each of you His holiness and His Divine Spirit. How blessed you are, my children.

You are my Son's blessed people. You are His holy ones. That is why I ask you to persevere, have strength and always remain in your faith.

These words are encouragement for you because I know the plan my Jesus has for you! He loves you beyond your deepest recognition. He loves you, my dear children, and I, your mother and mistress, adore Him in your name!

PRAISE BE MY JESUS. HE IS YOUR JESUS OF MERCY!

OCTOBER 5, 1989
(MARY)

My dear children, I, your mother, am so pleased to see how you are reconciling with your fellow brothers. I am pleased with your openness and loving embraces. Thank you for your effort, my dear ones.

When you are open, you allow my Jesus to convert your hearts to the way He created them! He is by your side, guiding you, especially in your weakest moments of vulnerability! Continue to walk with Us in openness and honesty. All else shall be taken care of for you!

Remember, a healthy soul overcomes all ailments. Thank you for your response to my call.

OCTOBER 12, 1989
(MARY)

My dear children, this night I wish for you to focus on my Son.

Do not look at yesterday or anticipate tomorrow. Do not speak of the things and events that cause distraction or harm in your conversion! SPEAK OF THE GOOD AND PEACEFUL EVENTS. DO NOT DWELL ON CHASTISEMENT OR THE EVENTS TO COME. DWELL ON PEACE AND PEACE WILL COME!

You are the instruments through which conversion is seeded in my Son's people, my children. I wish my children to come back to my Son through love and peace, not because fear is instilled in them from what may not come. Speak of goodness and be loving always.

Please, hear and listen to my words with obedience. I wish all of you, who have been converted to my Son's tender heart, to convert others through love and speaking of peace and goodness, as you were called. DO NOT BLOCK YOUR CONVERSION BY DWELLING ON THE INCORRECT SUBJECT! PEACE IS THE SUBJECT, AND LOVE AND MERCY; NOT WARS, DISASTERS, OR THE CHASTISEMENT!

Thank you, my dear ones, for responding seriously to this call.

OCTOBER 19, 1989
(MARY)

My dear children, always thank God for the many blessings of life He has granted you. Continuously give Him praise and thanks. Contemplate His goodness, for Our Father is a gracious and most loving God.

If Jesus gives to you a life of everlasting happiness and peace, think of the goodness and blessedness of Our God, through Whom all goodness and gifts of beauty are created!

Thank Him, for He gave to you the key to everlasting life...His Son, your Jesus! Blessed be Jesus and blessed be His children, created by the Eternal One on High, for they are one with Him!

OCTOBER 26, 1989
(MARY)

My dear children, you are the little children of God. Please use your gifts of faith, trust and hope. They are such powerful graces bestowed upon you in the eyes of God. Please have confidence in Him and trust emphatically.

Your faith is your comfort! The more you trust, the more you shall be comforted! God will care for you. He has all this time, and shall not stop providing.

DO NOT ALLOW ANYONE TO DISRUPT YOUR FOCUS AND TRUST FOR MY SON. Walk with Him and trust with all confidence in His divine care. He shall comfort you through the grace of your faith.

Thank you, my little children, for your response to my call, a call for peace and happiness!

NOVEMBER 9, 1989
(OUR LORD)

My dear people, love the ones you dislike! When they hurt you, pray for them. I will give you My peace and compassion. With My compassion, you will be able to forgive them and you will have My mercy for them. You will love them with My love, a love which embraces the soul.

I loved My enemies and I still love the ones who do not wish to know Me. It is My compassion that saves them. It is your compassion that will also save your enemies in My name and in My love.

I tell you, the day will come for you, who follow Me, when you will love your enemies with a love you never knew existed! You will love them greater than a dearest friend because it will be My love! Pray for the ones who befriend you. My glory, happiness and peace shall rest with you.

Thank you, My beloved ones, and My peace be with you!

NOVEMBER 23, 1989
(OUR LORD)

My dear people, know the time of My saving grace is at hand! My lessons, once available to the world, shall commence

My grace period, allowed by My Father to gather My good! The good shall be weeded from the bad for no man gathers fruitless crops from His harvest!

TAKE HEED, MY PEOPLE, AND KNOW OF MY GREAT LOVE FOR YOU. TRUST IN ME!

Trusting in Me is living in Me as one Spirit. Trust in yourselves by trusting in Me as I trust in you! There are many blessings I wish to give to you, many endless gifts which await you, graces of life!

Say, 'yes' to your Jesus and say, 'yes' to eternal life!

NOVEMBER 30, 1989
(MARY)

My dear children, do not be discouraged. My Jesus is here for you!

It is difficult to convince people to accept and trust in my Son's truth, because there are so few who love Him. But do not be discouraged. Your love and actions will set the precedence for their conversion. Simply pray for all and you will be saved! I cannot stress enough to you the seriousness of your prayers.

THE ANTICHRIST IS ALIVE AND WISHES TO DECEIVE YOU! Pray to my Jesus. He loves you and will protect you. The Antichrist is weak and he wishes for you to think that you are weak! Know that all who follow and walk with my Son are powerful because they receive the Father's zeal of power and strength.

Remember, those who walk with my Jesus are not weak. It is the demons who are weak. NEVER, NEVER FORGET WHAT I HAVE TOLD YOU!

Peace, my loved ones, and thank you for responding to my call!

DECEMBER 14, 1989
(MARY)

My dear children, this day my Son has gathered into His most tender heart all of those you have prayed for in love! Prayer is the key to all success.

The success of my plan relies on your prayer and devotion to my Son! Please, continue to pray and live in His faith. It will successfully end in your salvation. YOU GAIN HIS POWER THROUGH PRAYER!

Thank you, my dear ones, and know I continually pray for you!

DECEMBER 21, 1989
(MARY)

My dear children, love your Jesus with all of your heart as He loves you! Take pride in loving His loved ones, for all belong to Him.

Love and sincerity are the key to eternal glory. You have the gift of love because you have my Son! Please, use this gift, especially now, during this celebration of His birth. I promise you, your soul will rejoice!

Celebrate with me, for Our Saviour is here and He is yours. Rejoice and be glad. Know Him, my dear ones. Know Him intimately, for He is here for each one of you.

Peace, my dear ones. Peace for all eternity for you, my children of the Americas!

DECEMBER 25, 1989
(MARY)

My dear children, the kings came from afar to pay homage to our King, and today He, your King, comes to bring you hope and happiness. He is your sweet Jesus!

Please, my dear ones, know the way of my Son. Practice His ways and unite with Him. He brings you tidings of joy.

Pray, pray, pray to your beloved God of Hosts. Pray, and live according to His way.

It is so necessary to receive His graces. Begin once again, this day, my dear ones. Commence the new decade with mercy! Thank you for responding to my call.

DECEMBER 28, 1989
(MARY)

My dear children, it is glorious that my Son has allowed me to come here. Live your lives for Him, as I.

My dear, dear children, I am your Mother of Mercy. I have come here to the Americas to bring my children back to my Son. His mercy is upon you. I wish for all to be glorified in Him. It is all possible through desire and prayer.

Always pray, and the Divine Father shall replenish you with abundant gifts. Love one another always. Love all of different faiths. Never deny anyone your love, for all belong to the Father! Never condemn! Always, always, love. Be patient and peaceful children.

Thank you for responding to my call.

JANUARY 11, 1990
(MARY)

My dear children, it pleases me to see your hearts devoted to my Son. You love Him dearly. It is my wish now for you to allow my Jesus to love you. It is He Who desires to give to you. Always pray and be open to Him.

In these days, it is so necessary to focus intently on prayer and the love my Son has for you. Live in His faith always and never despair. All that He has promised will be fulfilled! Have faith in what He has told you, for it will be done according to the word of His law!

Thank you, my dear ones, for your response to my call.

JANUARY 18, 1990
(MARY)

My dear children, pray in thanksgiving to my Son for allowing me to come here! He is your beloved Master and Saviour. He is the only way to true happiness, peace and comfort. Please, trust in Him.

You are still frightened and wish to control. Trust in my Son! Please, practice His ways and cease your arguments! Be open-hearted and loving people. This is truly necessary in order for you to accommodate the many to come here.

IT IS YOUR LOVE THEY NEED AND YOUR WELCOME, AS I WELCOME AND LOVE ALL WHO COME TO THIS, MY SON'S CENTER OF MERCY! Jesus has blessed you with me so, please, thank Him by showing others love. Thank you for responding to my call.

JANUARY 25, 1990
(MARY)

My dear children, always be loving, open and honest. This is so necessary in order for you to relay my messages to those who come here, exactly as they are, without adding or subtracting from them.

Always be loving, and you shall receive the joy you bring my Son. This joy is endless and brings glory.

Thank you, my dear ones, for your response to my call.

VOLUME II

Part III

Messages
From Our Lord and Our Lady

As Given Through
The Homily At
Thursday Night Liturgy

Note:
Since all the words in these messages are
those of Our Lord, or Our Lady, quotation
marks are thus eliminated.

Messages From Our Lord and Our Lady Given Through Thursday Night Homily

JULY 6, 1989

(MARY)

It gives me great joy to be with you this night as you honor my Son under the title of His Mercy. Ask Him and Our Eternal Father to be with you. My Jesus under His title of Mercy will also be here! Come to Him, my dear ones. My heart overflows with joy at how much He loves, and how much He loves you, each of you!

Our Eternal Father has allowed both of Us to be with you. This will be a center of my Jesus' mercy for all who come. As they come, my dear ones, whether you understand or not, you are prepared to receive all of these ones. Have mercy on them, and my Jesus will have mercy on you.

He is shedding His mercy upon you now. As you come to Him, do not fear to hope, for He has great hope for you!

I take you, my dear ones, into my heart this night and present you to my Jesus of Mercy with His heart overflowing with love and forgiveness for those who ask! We will always be with you until the time when We come to take you home! Until that time, know that this is your home, because this is where His mercy and my peace dwell for you.

Thank you for honoring my Son. Thank you, my dear ones. Peace! Peace!

JULY 13, 1989

(OUR LORD)

I have had so much hope for you, My dear ones, and now I come to you and I, your Lord, plead with you: 'EMBRACE YOUR CROSS, PLEASE, DO NOT SHUN YOUR CROSS!'

Do you think it was easy for Me to bear the Cross for you? I gladly did it for love of you, and in obedience to My Father. I beg you, embrace your cross in reparation for your sins. You have no idea how your sins continue to grieve Me.

I love you. Please, love Me! I want you with Me. You need to make reparation for your sins. My mother grieves for you and pleads for you. The time is truly short!

I beg you, listen to Me or listen to My mother, but...LISTEN! My Eternal Father has sent Us to you.

I died in love. Please, My dear ones, live for Me in reparation for your sins and in love. I promise to be with you always.

JULY 20, 1989
(OUR LORD)

My dear ones, I, your Lord, do offer you this night My comfort and My peace. The words of My gospel message are true. My yoke is easy and My burden light, because I never give you a task, a cross, or a burden, without also being there with you every step of your way!

My dear ones, I am your way! Allow Me to journey with you, and you will be free and peace-filled. I offer you life...My Life! I invite you to accept that gift. Come to Me as you are weary, and I truly will give you refreshment. Come to Me when you feel lonely, and I will be with you.

You give Me so much joy! You are responding. Continue to respond in love, no matter how difficult the road. I am with you, and I give you My mother, also.

Take Our hand, and We will lead you to the Kingdom of My Father!

AUGUST 10, 1989
(OUR LORD)

My dear ones, My dear mother is honored by Myself and by My Father, because of her obedience. This obedience did not come from her human understanding, but from her spouse, Our Holy Spirit.

I give her to you this night as an example of the kind of obedience I invite you to give to Me, and to her, and to Our Heavenly Father. Because of her obedience, she was able to pray: 'My soul magnifies the Lord, and My spirit rejoices in God, My Saviour.'

My dear ones, the gift of your obedience is the gift of your heart to Me. When you obey Me, I take that gift and present it to My Father. It is because of your obedience that many, many graces are being shed upon you at this place at this time. And because of your obedience, you are causing that grace to overflow onto all those who come to you!

My Father allows Me to come to thank you for your obedience. I take you into My heart again, this night, in gratitude for that gift, and I leave My mother with you as My physical sign and example to you of the obedience that is most pleasing to My Father. Continue, My dear ones, to cherish her as she so cherishes you!

You are allowing her, because of your obedience, to lead you to Me. I give you My mercy and My love. *(Hands held out toward assembly.)* Live on in My Peace. *(Hands and arms extended up over assembly!)*

AUGUST 17, 1989
(OUR LORD)

My dear ones, Our Holy Spirit has been always with you from the very beginning of your time here on earth, prompting you, guiding you, protecting you and sanctifying you. Our Spirit was the gift We gave you, and it is the gift that I give you again this night!

Receive again, Our Holy Spirit. Through that Spirit, I your Lord, touch your heart this night. Allow Me to melt your heart if it is closed and cold. Allow Me to open it, and to pour My mercy this night upon you. Give Me your heart, and I will take it and put it in My heart, and there Our Father will see you in Me.

My dear ones, allow this blessing to happen! Give Me that gift, so that My mercy and the gift of Our Holy Spirit may flow to you, healing, forgiving and sanctifying.

I love you. I will always love you! I, your Lord, will never give up on you...NEVER, NEVER, NEVER!

AUGUST 24, 1989 *(None given for this date)*

AUGUST 31, 1989
(MARY)

My dear little children, you are my holy ones! I thank you for your prayers, and I invite you this night to more prayer. Honor my Son with your prayer. Pray for peace, please. Pray that your heart may continue to be converted.

I see your weariness, little ones. Please, I invite you not to give up, but to continue in your prayer. Your prayer is so vital to me and for your world. DON'T GIVE UP. CONTINUE!

Believe me when I say it is because of your prayer that I, your mother, am allowed to be with you in so many ways for so long a time. This, truly, is the time of my Son's grace. Never stop allowing Him to work through you.

I promise, little ones, to come whenever you invite me! It is the joy of my heart when you invite me, your mother, to pray with you to my Son and our Saviour, Jesus.

Thank you for your prayers and for trying so hard to love! Your attempts do not go unnoticed. Thank you, my little ones, my little holy ones. I love you!

SEPTEMBER 7, 1989
(OUR LORD)

My dear ones, why don't you trust in My care for you? I extend always, My mercy and love to you.

My Father sent Me to you, not to frighten you, but only to love you. Why do you still hesitate to trust? I ask for your obedience. Is it such a difficult request? I long for your heart. Can't you see that when you give Me your heart, I can fill it with My mercy and love? I long to do that!

I ask you, again, listen and obey, and I will be able to present you to My Father, and flood you with My mercy.

I love you with all My heart. I beg you, trust Me!

SEPTEMBER 14, 1989
(OUR LORD)

My dear ones, I ask you, this night, not to run away from the cross. As you look on My Cross, remember My obedience to My Father.

Please, My dear ones, I beg you not to be fearful of the cross! It was the instrument that gave you life and that gave Me life! The cross is to be embraced. It is not to be run from. Embrace My Cross in your lives, and know that when you do so, you are embracing Me!

The way of Acceptance is THROUGH OBEDIENCE. Obedience leads through death to life. Why else would you celebrate the triumph of an instrument of destruction? Because of My obedience to My Father, He turned the instrument of destruction into the way for life eternal with Him.

My dear ones, I offer you, this night, a share of My Cross. For each one of you, it will be manifested in a different way. But it is My Cross! I ask you, accept it! Embrace it! For as you accept it and embrace it, you accept Me and embrace Me. I will be with you. I promise to be with you, as you share with Me the cross of redemption and life.

My Cross is the sign of My love for you. Embracing My Cross will be a sign of your love for Me, and My Father, Who glorified My Cross, will also glorify yours! HE LOVES US SO MUCH.

OCTOBER 12, 1989
(OUR LORD)

My dear ones, I want to thank you for your persistence in prayer. I say again that not one of your prayers goes unheard, or goes undelivered to My heavenly Father.

I, this night, encourage you to continue in your prayer for peace, for conversion, and for My Divine Mercy. Those gifts I gladly give to you so that, in turn, you may give them to My little ones who are still so lost. The desire of My heart is to have all of them with Me.

Please, pray for them, gather them for Me. I use you as My hands and My arms and My heart. Embrace them and it will be Me embracing them! I thank you and I love you and I give you My Spirit.

OCTOBER 19, 1989
(OUR LORD)

My dear ones, when you pray for My mercy, as you have done so lovingly this night, it melts My heart. I cannot describe the love that I give to you this night, as you pray for My mercy.

I beg you, My dear ones, do not stop praying for My mercy. It is truly My joy to give it to you, and to all those for whom you pray. My joy overflows upon you this night. The tenderness with which I gather you in My arms is so much like the tenderness that My mother constantly has for you.

Your prayers of mercy are answered. You have captured My heart! I love you so.

I ask you now, you who have My mercy, be merciful to all of them whom I send you each day. As they experience My mercy through you, their hearts will likewise be melted and they will no longer be afraid to come to Me themselves. Look at what you have done for Me, your Lord! I thank you and I love you and I give you now, My peace. Know, from this moment on, that My peace is with you always.

My mother sends her love to you this night as she continues to pray with you. Oh, My dear ones, how she and I love you! Remember, however, that Our love is simply the reflection of the love that Our Father, My Father, has for each of you, His adopted loved ones!

OCTOBER 26, 1989
(OUR LORD)

My dear ones, I come to you this night to tell you what an effect you have had, and still have, on Me, your Lord. When I came to you the first time, I did not intend to bring dissension, and yet, I saw that the more I spoke the truth, the more the people resisted it. I say to you, I do not come this time to bring dissension, but to bring truth and salvation.

Still, My children look upon Me, their Saviour and upon My Father, Who is their God, with hearts that are not open, because you are still judging, even judging yourself in your relationship with Me! I have called you My friends to show you what freedom I give to you and what respect I have for you, each of you.

PLEASE BELIEVE IN THE VALUE OF YOUR LIFE. PLEASE BELIEVE HOW MUCH I LOVE YOU AND WANT YOU TO FOLLOW ME. I want you to follow as a friend, not as a slave! I beg you, do not be slaves to the evil one, to your pride, to your selfishness!

I give you My strength and My love to overcome the power of the evil one. I ask you, again this night, to use the power of My Spirit within you, so that you may experience the peace and the joy and the love of My own heart! I want so much for each of you to be in My heart!

NOVEMBER 30, 1989
(MARY)

My dear children, I, your mother, invite you again this night, to follow my Son. I encourage you to continue to pray with your hearts. You are seeing in your world the power of prayer! DO NOT GIVE UP! Your prayer, united to mine, is more powerful than Satan!

My dear ones, rededicate yourself, this night, to prayer. My heart is so full of gratitude. I thank you. I love you. I am with you, thanks to the love my Son has for each of you.

Be at peace. Receive the grace of my Son.

DECEMBER 2, 1989
(OUR LORD)

I give you My holy mother, My dear ones; this now is her season. I give her to you as the sample of how I invite you to respond to My call.

My dear ones, never think that honoring My mother brings dishonor to Me! WHEN YOU SEE MY MOTHER, YOU SEE ME! How it saddens My heart that so many of My children reject My mother. Don't they know that when they reject her, they are rejecting My heart. I LOVE HER SO!

I invite you to love her, for she loves you with her Immaculate Heart. I rejoice this night because of her and if I, your Lord, honor her, why do My children not follow My example? Take her hand, honor her, love her, and she will lead you to Me.

I give you My peace. I give you My heart. Cherish these gifts until I return to you.

DECEMBER 28, 1989

My dear ones, I am with you and I give you My peace! Listen, listen to My words... *(sermon from Father Jack followed.)*

On this feast of the Holy Innocents, the Lord wants us to know that this feast reminds us of how misuse of free will can destroy others. Parents' misuse of free will destroyed the infants. You and I need to be so careful now, and realize how the use of our free will destroys our relationship with God in so many ways, damaging it in so many ways, and hurting others in ways that, maybe, we will never know.

They give us the strength to not misuse our free will! They invite us now, to recommit ourselves to Them, asking for Their help to respond to Their grace, so that we will not misuse our free will. Our Lady asks us to intensify our prayer during these next days; to pray even more earnestly, and with our heart, for those most in need of Their mercy.

I invite you between now, the 28th of December and the 1st of January, to fast, as much as we can, to the extent that we, as individuals, are able. We are all different because of where we are, but, we need to fast for those most in need of God's mercy; to fast also for ourselves, so that we would be cleansed a little bit more of those things that are tempting us to misuse our free will!

I invite you to do that as a gift for yourself and a gift for Them. Again, I say, fast according to your ability. If it's not being able to fast on bread and water, or being able to fast from any kind of food because of your health, then fast from something else, offering that to Them between now and the 1st of January.

They want us, truly, to rededicate ourselves, even more, to prayer. They want us to listen more intently to Them speaking to our hearts. They love us so much and They are so present to us. We, who for whatever reason, come to pray,

have been called to that prayer and we pray, not only for ourselves, but for the rest of the world.

She wants you to know how serious that is, and to take
it seriously, not somberly, but seriously. She loves you and
me very, very much and Our Lord is here, as He said, with
His mercy. Our prayer (and I don't understand this, I'm just
saying it) our prayer releases His mercy upon those for whom
we pray. That is how powerful our prayer is and that is how
much He respects us and needs us!

I want to say to you, thank you for responding to that call.
Your prayer has made, already, a significant difference in our
world. Don't be blinded to what is happening. God loves you
very much. I don't want you to ever forget that, and They
love you.

JANUARY 4, 1990
(OUR LORD)

My dear loved ones, with all My heart, I invite you to come
and to see your Lord!

I, Who dwell always in the tabernacle, am always present
to you in the tabernacle of the altar and in the tabernacle
of your heart! It is My wish, the wish of your Lord, that
you would begin to appreciate My real presence in both of
those tabernacles!

Please believe Me, My dear ones. I am as truly present
in the tabernacle of your heart as I am truly present in the
tabernacle of this altar! That is how much I love you.

I come to dwell within you, and when I come to dwell
within you, I bring with Me My Most Holy Father and Our
Most Holy Spirit. You are the tabernacle of Our Life! I beg
you, My dear ones, to hold sacred, as I do, the tabernacle
of your heart.

Treasure My presence within you. I AM ALWAYS WITH
YOU. There is nothing at all to be afraid of. Be at peace,
and know that I, your Lord, love you and consecrate you to
My Father.

JANUARY 11, 1990
(OUR LORD)

My dear ones, I, your Lord, wish to heal you. I, your Lord, wish to make you whole again. Allow Me that freedom in your heart. I want to tell you how you limit My love for you, how you block what I long to do for you.

COME TO ME WITH OPEN HEART, WITH OPEN MIND. PLACE YOURSELF BEFORE ME IN MY SACRAMENT, AND THEN I WILL BE ABLE TO HEAL YOU AS I WISH!

Please believe Me, please trust in Me, that I, your Lord, know how and when and what you most need healing in! It is My mercy and My love that I wish to pour upon you. These are the healing graces that are yours. If you only allow Me to give them to you!

Present to Me this night your heart, and I will embrace it and draw it nearer to Mine; and there you will feel My mercy and My healing and My love. You will be filled with joy, the joy that I wish to give you.

Please, My dear ones, believe Me when I say, 'I love you with all of My heart.'

JANUARY 18, 1990
(OUR LORD)

My dear ones, I beg you, this night, to overcome your jealousy. Don't you realize, that when you are jealous of another, you disregard the gift that My Father has given to you? I tell you again, there is no gift greater than another gift. Each gift comes from My Father.

I ask you this night, allow Me, your Saviour and Lord, to heal jealousy in your heart, so that I can give you a new heart. Rejoice in the gift that I give you, My merciful love. Look upon the gifts of your brothers and sisters and be thankful for them, thankful to the Spirit, thankful to My Father.

I beg you to resign your jealousy, and use the gifts that you have to touch those whom I will send you, if you allow Me. I will give you My mercy for them. It will be My mercy, through you, if you only allow it!

Know that I love you and that I want for you joy.

JANUARY 25, 1990
(OUR LORD)

My dear ones, what I say to you this night, I ask you to listen to carefully.

Because you are My disciples, you will suffer. Because you are saying, 'yes,' and allowing My Father and Myself and Our Spirit to convert you, you will suffer.

As you spread our good news of joy, peace and hope to the world, you will be ridiculed. You will be laughed at and you will suffer. I tell you this night, My dear ones, that through all of that suffering, I AM WITH YOU. I SEND MY MOTHER TO BE WITH YOU.

And so I say to you, do not fear suffering because I can take that and redeem many! I thank you for saying, 'yes,' for taking the risk in believing, in loving, in touching those whom I send to you.

I give you this night a blessing, the sign of My Cross on your heart, a sign that contradicted the world. The sign of suffering is turned into eternal joy.

This is what I will do with your suffering. I will turn it into joy as you give it to Me.

I love you. Bear all!

THE RIEHLE FOUNDATION...

The Riehle Foundation is a non-profit, tax-exempt, charitable organization that exists to produce and/or distribute Catholic material to anyone, anywhere.

The Foundation is dedicated to the Mother of God and her role in the salvation of mankind. We believe that this role has not diminished in our time, but, on the contrary has become all the more apparent in this the era of Mary as recognized by Pope John Paul II, whom we strongly support.

During the past two years the foundation has distributed over one million books, films, rosaries, bibles, etc. to individuals, parishes, and organizations all over the world. Additionally, the foundation sends materials to missions and parishes in a dozen foreign countries.

Donations forwarded to The Riehle Foundation for the materials distributed provide our sole support. We appreciate your assistance, and request your prayers.

IN THE SERVICE OF JESUS AND MARY
All for the honor and glory of God!

The Riehle Foundation
P.O. Box 7
Milford, OH 45150